"Scott Morton has done us a favor. He has taken one of the most profound topics in the Bible and simplified it. Anyone serious about being used of God to make disciples of all nations will find *Down-to-Earth Discipling* a true gift from God."

—Dr. LeRoy Eims, The Navigators;
author, *The Lost Art of Disciplemaking*

"Instead of seeking to have an influence on a large number of people for Christ, we need to give our attention to one person at a time. That is the way the gospel spreads from one to another—it's as simple as that! Scott has brought us back to the basics in this book and we need to hear what he is saying."

—Dr. John H. Stevens, pastor,
First Presbyterian Church, Colorado Springs, Colorado

"Scott Morton does us all a great service: He makes discipling doable. You can make it part of normal life. Sixty years of discipling tells me that following Scott's suggestions will result in an exceptionally rewarding personal ministry. I highly recommend *Down-to-Earth Discipling.*"

—Lorne Sanny, president emeritus, The Navigators

"Few people can communicate in a down-to-earth, practical manner, as Scott Morton so ably does. He demonstrates his ability to connect with the world of the average Christian to engage him in the vital arena of discipling."

—Ellis F. Goldstein, director of Ministry Partner
Development, Campus Crusade for Christ

"As a pastor, I want to know if a writer really knows his subject firsthand. Has he himself field-tested his counsel? Scott has, and that's where I found him at his best."

—Reverend James E. Olson, D.Min., senior pastor,
Faith Evangelical Free Church, Fort Collins, Colorado

"When I was doing cartoons for Scott, he would send stick-figure sketches of his ideas to get me going in the right direction. But you'll find no stick figures in *Down-to-Earth Discipling.* Scott's clear descriptions of what to do and how to do it show the way very nicely."

—Wayne Stayskal, editorial cartoonist, *Tampa Tribune*

DOWN TO EARTH DISCIPLING

Essential Principles to Guide Your Personal Ministry

SCOTT MORTON

NAVPRESS

Bringing Truth to Life
P.O. Box 35001, Colorado Springs, Colorado 80935

OUR GUARANTEE TO YOU

We believe so strongly in the message of our books that we are making this quality guarantee to you. If for any reason you are disappointed with the content of this book, return the title page to us with your name and address and we will refund to you the list price of the book. To help us serve you better, please briefly describe why you were disappointed. Mail your refund request to: NavPress, P.O. Box 35002, Colorado Springs, CO 80935.

The Navigators is an international Christian organization. Our mission is to reach, disciple, and equip people to know Christ and to make Him known through successive generations. We envision multitudes of diverse people in the United States and every other nation who have a passionate love for Christ, live a lifestyle of sharing Christ's love, and multiply spiritual laborers among those without Christ.

NavPress is the publishing ministry of The Navigators. NavPress publications help believers learn biblical truth and apply what they learn to their lives and ministries. Our mission is to stimulate spiritual formation among our readers.

Cover design by Dan Jamison
Cover photograph from Image State
Creative Team: Don Simpson, Jacqueline Eaton Blakley, Darla Hightower, Laura Spray

Some of the anecdotal illustrations in this book are true to life and are included with the permission of the persons involved. All other illustrations are composites of real situations, and any resemblance to people living or dead is coincidental.

Unless otherwise identified, all Scripture quotations in this publication are taken from the *New American Standard Bible* (NASB), © The Lockman Foundation 1960, 1962, 1963, 1968, 1971, 1972, 1973, 1975, 1977. Other versions used include: the HOLY BIBLE: NEW INTERNATIONAL VERSION® (NIV®), Copyright © 1973, 1978, 1984 by International Bible Society, used by permission of Zondervan Publishing House, all rights reserved; and the *King James Version* (KJV).

Morton, Scott.
  Down-to-earth discipling : essential principles to guide your personal
ministry / Scott Morton.
      p. cm.
Includes bibliographical references.
  ISBN 1-57683-339-9
  1. Discipling (Christianity) I. Title.
  BV4520 .M64 2003
  253--dc21
                            2002014318

Printed in the United States of America

1 2 3 4 5 6 7 8 9 10 / 07 06 05 04 03

Contents

Preface

I FEAR MANY CHRISTIAN LAY LEADERS ARE GIVING UP.

Take my friend Jack, for example. Jack lives in a river town in the Midwest. In the past, he had a great heart for God and a passion for reaching spiritually hungry people one by one with the gospel. He didn't get involved in splashy evangelistic programs. He preferred to befriend the people he met daily as a resident "insider"—someone who lives out the gospel and spreads it naturally, not in an apostolic or confrontational manner.

But Jack's church grabbed him for leadership. And they should have: he served well. And both he and his wife Donna got busy in demanding careers and are raising a growing family. But they are tired. Over the last five years Jack and Donna have drifted from trying to engage nonbelievers in the gospel. They hang out mostly with believers. It's easier.

They are also lonely. They get no affirmation from anyone who understands their ministry dreams. Jack told me, "I feel like a lonely ember on the far end of the fireplace. All the fire has burned away from me. I am alone—still glowing, but getting cooler every year."

This book is dedicated to thousands of Christ-centered laborers who once dared to dream that they could multiply among the lost. I beseech you—don't give up. I believe I have found ways—mostly by trial and error—that will reenergize you and help you become effective in ministry right where you are. Read on!

CHAPTER ONE

Your Secret Asset in Ministry

YOU POSSESS A POWERFUL SECRET RESOURCE FOR MINISTRY. It can open the hearts of Christian friends; it can melt the skepticism of nonbelievers. And it reduces the size of your personal problems. It is readily at hand—you can use it whenever you are around people.

Is it intercessory prayer? No, though that is indispensable. Is it your spiritual gifts? No, but those are helpful. Is it finding a dynamic church? No, but it helps to have a team of likeminded friends. Furthermore, you needn't go to seminary or a retreat to learn to use your hidden asset.

What is it? Here is a clue from Colin Powell, speaking to the National Endowment for the Humanities in Washington, D.C., in 1999. He pleaded with the delegates to help economically deprived young people, but warned, "It's more than just throwing computers at them." He went on to explain that organizing programs is not enough. Powell asked people to spend quality time with youngsters—to give them *personal attention one by one*. The result?

> You should see those kids being tutored by old,
> retired geezers at my church. And suddenly these kids
> are saying, "White people are not enemies—look at
> them; they spend their Saturday mornings with me."

What is your secret ministry asset? The power of *personal attentiveness.* Colin Powell understands that *programs* alone cannot bring lasting change, but personal attention to people one by one can make the difference of a lifetime.

Do we have the same understanding in Christian ministry? There is no shortage of Christian programs in the U.S. On any given weekend believers can find seminars on church growth, spiritual formation, leadership skills, discovering one's spiritual gifts, handling money, and rejuvenating marriages. All helpful.

But despite the multiplication of good teaching, good books, good videos, and good churches, research shows we are not penetrating the culture with the gospel. Frankly, we are not much different from the nonChristian culture we seek to save. A manager of a large hotel told me the hotel sells more in-room pornographic movies during Christian conventions than any others!

The kingdom of God needs more than programs. We need a massive dose of millions of believers demonstrating *personal attentiveness.* We seem not to realize the power one life can have on another. Proverbs 27:17 says it best: "As iron sharpens iron, so one man sharpens another" (NIV). The picture here is of a farm implement—metal rubbing against metal and becoming sharper in the process, like sharpening a knife. But notice that *iron* sharpens *iron.* Creampuffs do not sharpen creampuffs! Pillows do not sharpen pillows! Gummy bears do not sharpen gummy bears! Furthermore, iron can't sharpen iron from a distance—iron must touch iron! In the same way, people can sharpen one another only if they are in close proximity—close enough to "rub."

The Shoe Store Clerk
When personal attentiveness is added to a "program," the results can be powerful. Not many of us have heard of Edward Kimball. (No, not Richard Kimble, "The TV Fugitive," who spent a half-hour each week in the 1960s

searching for a one-armed man.) He taught a Sunday school class for young working men in Boston. In the midst of revival services at his church program, Kimball left his lodging at America House on Saturday morning, April 21, 1855, impressed that the Lord wanted him to speak to one of his students employed as a shoe clerk. He describes his visit to Holton's shoe store:

> I thought maybe my mission might embarrass the boy, that when I went away the other clerks might ask who I was, and when they learned might taunt [him] and ask if I was trying to make a good boy out of him. While I was pondering over it all I passed the store without noticing it. Then when I found I had gone by the door I determined to make a dash for it and have it over at once.[1]

Not exactly a bold leader! Nonetheless, Kimball found the young clerk in the back wrapping shoes in paper and stacking them on shelves. Kimball continued: "I went up to him and put my hand on his shoulder, and as I leaned over I placed my foot upon a shoe box."[2] There were tears in Kimball's eyes as he told the young man about Christ, "who loved him and who wanted his love." Kimball recalled afterward that it was quite a weak plea, and he could not remember the exact words he used. But the young clerk received Jesus Christ that very hour.

No one remembers Edward Kimball, but most of us have heard of the young shoe store clerk—D. L. Moody! The personal attentiveness of Edward Kimball multiplied over the next forty-five years to millions of people through the worldwide preaching of D. L. Moody.

Though Moody attended church services, that is not where he came to Christ. It was not even in Sunday school class—though both the class and the church services prepared him. It was not a program that reached Moody, but rather the one-to-one personal attentiveness of a fearful Sunday school teacher.

11

And Moody passed it on. In his crusades, Moody urged his "personal workers" (as he called them) to be patient and thorough in dealing with each inquirer: "No hurrying from one to another. Wait patiently and ply them with God's Word, and think, Oh! think what it is to win a soul for Christ, and don't grudge the time spent on one person."[3]

"Don't grudge the time spent on one person." Amazing! That is different from today's football-like, hurry-up evangelical offense whose playbook calls for filling large rooms with people, hoping they will attentively watch PowerPoint presentations.

This is not to say that group meetings are not important. Indeed, it was at a group event that I was prompted by the Holy Spirit to surrender to Christ. Both events and face-to-face encounters are needed. But group meetings don't inconvenience themselves to go downtown to a shoe store and win a clerk to Christ.

Ralph Waldo Emerson said it well:

> Let three of you come together and you shall not have one new and hearty word. Two may talk and one may hear, but three cannot take part in a conversation of the most sincere and searching sort.[4]

Jesus' Method

But one-to-one ministry is so slow. Why not teach many at a time? Saves time and money!

Yes, it is slow, but what are we measuring—bodies at a meeting house? Samuel Shoemaker said, "Disciples are not mass-produced; they are hewn out one by one."

What can you do? You know enough about walking with Christ to realize you must have an outlet—you know you must be a river, not a swamp. You know that your intimacy with Christ will shrivel if you're only a consuming spectator rather than a player on the field. Like me, you realize that when you share your life with others, your own problems seem to reduce in size. But where to start? You want to make a difference in people's lives personally—but how?

How did Jesus do it? Though He taught large groups and small groups, He knew the value of personal attentiveness with one person at a time. For example:

- He separated Peter from the other disciples to commission him to "tend my lambs" (John 21:15).
- He purposely sought out the blind man He had healed in order to follow up (John 9:35).
- He usually healed people one or two at a time—not in groups (though group healings would have helped more people and saved time).
- He singled out Thomas to reveal lack of faith. He singled out Zacchaeus in the tree, the woman with the issue of blood, Matthew at his tax desk, and James and John as they fished along the lake.

Jesus did much in groups, but *personal attentiveness* was a high value. And Jesus is not alone in His one-to-one approach. Examples of face-to-face personal attentiveness are scattered throughout the Bible.

- Jethro reproved Moses for the way he was leading (Exodus 18:13-23).
- In spite of great danger, Jonathan went to David to encourage him in God (1 Samuel 23:16).
- Moses charged Joshua—not a group, but one man—with the leadership of Israel (Deuteronomy 3:28).
- Aquila and Priscilla honed in on Apollos to explain "the way of God more perfectly" (Acts 18:24-28, KJV).

Where do you start? Don't volunteer for another committee. Don't ask to teach the biggest class at church. Begin with one person in your world who needs help.

Robert's Story

But will personal attentiveness make a difference today? It made a difference to Robert. I'd known Robert through mutual friends, and we connected frequently over several months. He was recently back from Germany, where he had served his military term and was looking for a job. He wondered whether I had a job to offer him.

"No, but let's get together and go over your résumé," I said, sounding more confident than I actually was! We met at a sandwich shop one noon and went over his résumé. That didn't take long, but we enjoyed getting better acquainted. Realizing I might not see him again because he might move soon, I asked if I could tell him about something that had made a big difference in my life—my spiritual journey. And I said I wanted to hear about his spiritual history, too. "OK," he said cautiously.

So I turned over the greasy placemat, took out my pen, and traced my spiritual journey using the bridge illustration (see appendix, page 152). I didn't preach. The response was silence. I felt a little like Edward Kimball—wanting to make a dash for it! "Robert, what's your spiritual background?" I heard a voice saying, not certain it was mine.

Robert smiled. "Not much," he said. "My dad never stayed around, but when he was home, this Jehovah's Witness guy kept stopping by. I read a little of his stuff. That's about it."

Silence.

"Could I take that diagram home?" Robert said, pointing to the placemat.

"Sure."

My next risk was suggesting we meet to read about the life of Jesus. He cautiously agreed, and we began getting together in his tiny duplex at 7 A.M. every second Tuesday. I'd bring three Burger King breakfast croissants—one for Robert, one for me, and one for his teenage son, who grabbed it on his way out the door heading for school.

At each of our meetings, Robert and I read one chapter of John's gospel and discussed it. No notes, no handouts, no sermonettes, no opening or closing prayers, no easy answers. Just Robert, me, the Bible, and the Holy Spirit.

I took my time. Robert turned out to be highly opinionated about Jehovah's Witnesses, the military, and women, to name three. I listened and tried to bring him back to John's text. Jesus was a mystery. I didn't pin him down to receive Christ, lest he make a premature decision.

After eight months Robert said he wasn't "good enough to receive Christ — got to make some changes first." True, Robert had some bad habits — smoking, drinking, cursing, and chasing women, for starters — but I had not railed against these during our breakfast studies. I kept the focus on Christ. He said, "Scott, in the mornings I get up and look under my car to see if I hit somebody while driving home drunk the night before."

I tried to explain that Christ changes a person over time and that no one has the willpower to change without God's help anyway. But Robert persisted: "Not good enough." Even Romans 5:8 ("while we were yet sinners") didn't help.

To my surprise, a few weeks later Robert asked if I thought a person could "do business with God on their smoke break." I raised up in my chair. "I took a smoke break at work last night . . . knew I needed to surrender . . . tears came. I couldn't stop crying, and I asked Jesus to come in."

Tears came to my eyes too. But that was just the beginning. Robert and I kept reading John together. Then I showed him how to memorize verses about assurance. I had moved from evangelism to discipling.

I tell this story to illustrate the power of personal attentiveness. There were half a dozen churches within a few blocks of Robert's duplex, but he didn't attend any of them. He had cable TV with a couple million channels, including religious ones, but he didn't tune in. Religious programs were advertised in our daily newspaper for single dads, but he didn't go. "Programs" were available, but it took my weak-kneed personal attentiveness to be the catalyst for Robert's finding Christ.

Edward Kimball—my hero! Soon Robert began attending the storefront church that had been there all the time. He was baptized and became active in their church programs, which supplied the momentum I could not supply one to one.

Neither programs nor personal attentiveness can thrive without the other, but in Christian ministry today we are overbalanced on the program side. We've got plenty of wonderful programs, but thousands of people like my friend Robert bypass these programs every day. Instead of expecting people to come to our programs, we need to go to them with loving one-to-one personal attentiveness. Once they see we care genuinely, once they see we have words of life, then they may take an interest in spiritual growth.

Can you make a difference? Why not ask God to give you one person to focus on? It may be a woman who rarely speaks up in Tuesday morning moms Bible study group. Maybe she doesn't have assurance of salvation. Or it may be a nonbeliever who would never darken the door of a church, but wouldn't think twice about joining you for lunch at a favorite sandwich shop.

But don't limit your personal attentiveness to only one lucky individual who is going to be your spiritual mentoree whether she likes it or not! Don't pick out "the one" just yet. Show attentiveness to many people—the new neighbor, the new assistant at work, the copier repair guy, the teen who babysits your kids, the mechanic who can't seem to find the problem with your transmission. (Perhaps the reason he can't find the problem is so that you will have opportunities to build a friendship with him!) Ask God to enable you to share your life with several people. He'll let you know when it is time to invite one to read the gospel of John with you.

Taking Responsibility

But isn't this already happening? With the success of so many Christian programs, aren't all seekers having their spiritual needs met? Unfortunately, the old adage is true: "Everyone's responsibility becomes no one's responsibility."

Years ago I took a group of college students to the beaches of Florida on a spring break trip. There were twelve of us in a 1953 Ford school bus, including Sydne, a newcomer to the group. On the return trip, we pulled away from a gas stop in a small Alabama town, and five miles down the road someone asked, "Where's Sydne?" She wasn't in the bus! I was driving and immediately screeched to a stop and made a U-turn. On the outskirts of town we found her running down the road toward us—crying uncontrollably. Not a good way to treat a newcomer!

What happened here? The eleven of us were a pretty close group—we were comfortable with one another and were not used to thinking outside ourselves. And not one of us took responsibility for Sydne. Because she was every one's responsibility, she was no one's responsibility. She never came to any more of our meetings.

The apostle Paul admonished the Corinthians:

> For if you were to have countless tutors in Christ, yet you would not have many fathers, for in Christ Jesus I became your father through the gospel.
> (1 Corinthians 4:15)

The Greek word translated "tutors" here is *paidagogos*. The *paidagogos* was a trainer of boys who exercised general supervision over his wards, often chastising them. Paul is drawing a distinction between "tutor" and "father." He says the Corinthians have countless tutors—many people who will chastise, criticize, and offer help—but who will be their father? A father feels more responsible than a *paidagogos*. A father cares more deeply for his "spiritual children"—praying for them, sacrificing for them, being vulnerable to them so they can see a model of how to live.

Today is no different. It is easy to "advise" everyone in the church, but it is harder to be a spiritual father or mother to *one* spiritually hungry seeker. So my question is this: You are busy with organizing programs, serving on committees . . . fine. But are you a spiritual father or mother to someone who is crying out to find intimacy with God?

Where's That One?

Dawson Trotman, founder of The Navigators, put it this way: "Where's your man? Where's your woman? Where's that one for whom you are pouring out your life to help them walk with Christ?" Your ministry can be more than attending endless meetings, more than being a tiny cog in a giant ministry. You can experience the joy of being used by God to touch one life. You can be the Edward Kimball for another believer.

But your pastor may object to your dropping out of the five committees you lead. He has a good point—leadership is needed. The programs don't run themselves. Try this: Limit yourself to faithfully serving in one "program" area. Do a good job and ask the pastor to send you to personally disciple others one to one.

Will you use the ministry asset you already possess— the gift of personal attentiveness—touching one life at a time? Don't be concerned now with who your person will be. Give personal attentiveness to many. God will give you at least one who will respond as you share your walk with Christ.

I've found that my own problems seem smaller when I actively share my life with someone learning to be a disciple. Perhaps you've discovered that too. I believe this is part of the answer to my friend Jack's problem that I discussed in the preface. The thrill of working with someone one to one—and seeing gradual but steady change— energizes us.

But there's a danger here! Will you feel fulfilled touching just one life rather than teaching a class of dozens? Or not having your name published in the list of class officers? Charles Spurgeon advised, "Those who loved you and were helped by you will remember you when forget-me-nots are withered. Carve your name on hearts and not on marble."

This poem by an anonymous author helps me remember that position and praise are not the goals:

> Father, where shall I work today?
> And my love flowed warm and free.
> Then He pointed out a tiny spot,
> And said, "Tend that for Me."
> I answered quickly, "Oh no, not that.
> Why no one would ever see,
> No matter how well my work was done,
> Not that little place for me!"
> And the word He spoke, it was not stern,
> He answered me tenderly,
> "Ah little one, search that heart of thine;
> Art thou working for them or Me?
> Nazareth was a little place,
> And so was Galilee."

What if Edward Kimball had decided to do only the things that would get noticed? As you give personal attentiveness to those God brings around you, you will have a ministry—and the results may surprise you. Dawson Trotman's question is still valid today: "Where's your man? Where's your woman?" It all starts with personal attentiveness.

CHAPTER TWO

Know Where You're Going: Three Stages of Personal Ministry

IT WAS 7 A.M. JERRY AND I WERE SITTING IN MY CHEVROLET in a church parking lot as a cold October rain pelted the windshield. I was showing him how to have a meaningful quiet time by doing it with him. The church lot was the only quiet place we could find halfway between his business and my home.

After we finished praying Jerry turned and thanked me for the thirty minutes. Then he asked, "Where is all this headed—our meeting together?" Silence. I froze, but my mind raced, *How do I answer? Why is he asking? Stall for time . . . 7:01.*

Jerry was a classic all-business, type-A personality and too eager, in my opinion, to get to the bottom line. Of course, I didn't have a clue, so I mumbled something about his finding out as we went along. Again, silence. I knew my answer didn't satisfy him, but it was the best I could do . . . 7:02. I should have said, "Good question! Next time we meet I'll show you a diagram with the answer." But I didn't.

Here's why Jerry's question is hard to answer: Jesus didn't give a specific formula for the discipling process. He told His followers to "make disciples." He said He would be with them to the end, and He modeled ministry values like love, service, and holiness. But a paint-by-numbers handbook? No.

Though Jesus gave no formula, we know three facts that encourage us to disciple others.

First, following Jesus propels us to "catch" others. He made no secret of that with Peter and Andrew: "Follow Me, and I will make you fishers of men." (Matthew 4:19). In His priestly prayer, Jesus revealed that He expected a third spiritual generation when He said: "I do not ask on behalf of these alone, but for those also who believe in Me through *their* word." (John 17:20, emphasis added). He never intended for His message to stop after two generations.

Second, He modeled *how* to disciple. By observing how He behaved with His disciples and what He taught (and didn't teach), we see how we should act with those we attempt to influence.

Third, Jesus left us the Comforter who guides us into all truth. I take great comfort in knowing that even though I am a channel God may use, the Holy Spirit does the work and I need only to stay in step with Him. It is not up to me.

So even without paint-by-numbers instructions, we have plenty to go on. At the risk of seeming formulaic, let me suggest that you can be more effective in personal discipling if you recognize three stages of ministry. But first a caution: these stages run together at the edges—you don't "graduate" from one stage to another. A laborer can have the same struggles as a new believer.

Stages of Personal Ministry

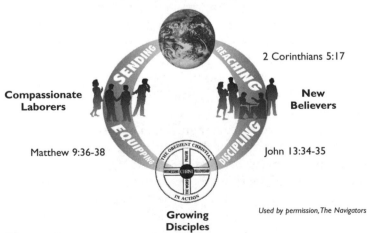

2 Corinthians 5:17

Compassionate Laborers

New Believers

Matthew 9:36-38

John 13:34-35

Growing Disciples

Used by permission, The Navigators

Here is how this overview of the ministry stages helps. Let's say you're leading a Bible study of six people, hoping they will become dedicated disciples of Christ. All six are in a different place in their spiritual journey. Perhaps you've encountered them in your personal ministry. For example:

- Bill is extremely likable; he loves the group but is quick to say he has no assurance of salvation; he comes to the study with Heineken on his breath.
- Katy, Bill's wife, earnestly seeks to lead others to Christ. Socially mature, she has a regular quiet time, loves the Bible, and speaks occasionally at a Christian women's club.
- Jasper wants to read the Bible but rarely does. He usually comes to the group unprepared. But he gives a wonderful testimony of his conversion as a teenager.
- Phil reads the Bible every day (actually, he has read through the Bible each year for nine years), but he is not Mr. Personality. He has few friends, even in the church. He's been a trustee for fourteen years and gives generously to missions.
- Julie (Phil's wife) has a big heart to know God and prays deep, wonderful prayers. She also leads a Bible study and talks often about her evangelism encounters.
- Gertrude loves God but is preoccupied with her church. She is on four committees but admits she doesn't get "fed" much except at your Bible study. She is fuzzy on the time of her commitment to Christ.

How will you disciple each one, given their differing spiritual journeys? Tailoring the Bible study to meet one person's need will miss another's need. Use the diagram to discern your next steps with each one. Like this:

Stages of Personal Ministry

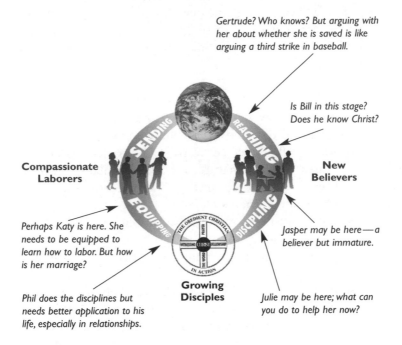

Gertrude? Who knows? But arguing with her about whether she is saved is like arguing a third strike in baseball.

Is Bill in this stage? Does he know Christ?

Compassionate Laborers

New Believers

Perhaps Katy is here. She needs to be equipped to learn how to labor. But how is her marriage?

Jasper may be here—a believer but immature.

Phil does the disciplines but needs better application to his life, especially in relationships.

Growing Disciples

Julie may be here; what can you do to help her now?

Placing people on a chart can feel artificial and dehumanizing. On the other hand, it can help you know what to do to help those you're discipling. This diagram also serves as your confidential prayer list. And remember, the three stages are not clearly delineated—they run together, and that is OK. Think in terms of "journey" or "process" as you minister, not crossing the line from one stage to the next.

To make the stages diagram even more helpful, identify the teachings or activities that meet the felt needs of your mentorees at each stage. On the following page I've listed several growth topics for each stage.

Stages of Personal Ministry: Topics to Share Next
(Add your own as needed.)

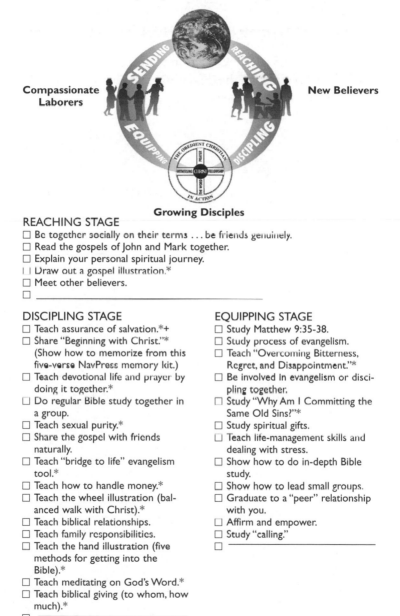

Compassionate Laborers

New Believers

Growing Disciples

REACHING STAGE
- ☐ Be together socially on their terms . . . be friends genuinely.
- ☐ Read the gospels of John and Mark together.
- ☐ Explain your personal spiritual journey.
- ☐ Draw out a gospel illustration.*
- ☐ Meet other believers.
- ☐ _____

DISCIPLING STAGE
- ☐ Teach assurance of salvation.*+
- ☐ Share "Beginning with Christ."* (Show how to memorize from this five-verse NavPress memory kit.)
- ☐ Teach devotional life and prayer by doing it together.*
- ☐ Do regular Bible study together in a group.
- ☐ Teach sexual purity.*
- ☐ Share the gospel with friends naturally.
- ☐ Teach "bridge to life" evangelism tool.*
- ☐ Teach how to handle money.*
- ☐ Teach the wheel illustration (balanced walk with Christ).*
- ☐ Teach biblical relationships.
- ☐ Teach family responsibilities.
- ☐ Teach the hand illustration (five methods for getting into the Bible).*
- ☐ Teach meditating on God's Word.*
- ☐ Teach biblical giving (to whom, how much).*
- ☐ _____

EQUIPPING STAGE
- ☐ Study Matthew 9:35-38.
- ☐ Study process of evangelism.
- ☐ Teach "Overcoming Bitterness, Regret, and Disappointment."*
- ☐ Be involved in evangelism or discipling together.
- ☐ Study "Why Am I Committing the Same Old Sins?"*
- ☐ Study spiritual gifts.
- ☐ Teach life-management skills and dealing with stress.
- ☐ Show how to do in-depth Bible study.
- ☐ Show how to lead small groups.
- ☐ Graduate to a "peer" relationship with you.
- ☐ Affirm and empower.
- ☐ Study "calling."
- ☐ _____

*See the appendix for sixty-minute pass-on-able studies you can do with a mentoree on this topic.
+Teach the gospel and its implications throughout the discipling-equipping stages too.

Let me emphasize again that the stages diagram is not a formula. I share it because mentorees are hindered unnecessarily when the disciplers (like me) don't know what to do next. I wish I had shared this diagram with Jerry that October day in the rain.

The next four chapters give important guidelines and warn of the pitfalls of the reaching stage, the discipling stage, and the equipping stage.

CHAPTER THREE

Stage One: Two Surprising Foundation Stones for Personal Evangelism

MANY BOOKS EXHORTING BELIEVERS TO DO EVANGELISM have been written by gifted evangelists. Though inspired by their stories of sharing the gospel, they make me tired. How can I match up? I am not a gifted evangelist. I'm even tempted to delegate my responsibility to share Christ to my pastor. (That's why we pay him, right?) Then the subtle pressure I feel when I'm around nonbelievers will be gone. Hallelujah!

More confession: I have become immune to exhortations to "share Christ!" Though I enjoy talking with people about the Lord once I get on the subject, I vacillate about initiating spiritual conversations. Even when it seems appropriate to ask a spiritual question, I find myself saying, "How 'bout them Packers!"

But then I can go to the other extreme. If a nonbeliever seems interested, I share my testimony, the four spiritual laws, the bridge illustration, and John 3:16, and for good measure I tell the story about the guy who went across Niagara Falls in a wheelbarrow. All in less than twenty minutes! Way too much.

In writing this chapter, I'm relying on the old baseball adage "Those who can't play, coach!" Casey Stengel and Tommy Lasorda had only mediocre records as major league players, but they became stellar managers. Good coaches break difficult tasks into components that can be observed and executed by ordinary players.

Similarly, you and I may not make the Hall of Fame in evangelism—but as we break out the biblical components of evangelism and faithfully plod under the leading of the Holy Spirit, we can become effective, and even coach others. In my own efforts, I am grateful to Jim Petersen, the late Paul Little, Josh McDowell, LeRoy Eims, and Mike Shamy, whose insights on evangelism have instructed me over the years. Many of my convictions originated with them.

Before we move to specific guidelines on how to relate to nonbelievers, we must correct two foundational misunderstandings about personal evangelism—otherwise, we risk painting primer over rotting wood.

Evangelism Is a Process—Not an Event

For years evangelicals have narrowed evangelism down to "reaping." We are disappointed if the agnostic we are sharing with does not pray the "sinner's prayer" within sixty minutes of hearing the gospel. True, now and then God has so prepared a seeker's heart that the individual will genuinely respond immediately. But this is not the norm. Most American adults do not come to Christ the first time they hear the gospel, but only after repeated exposure to it.

In my case, I had an "almost every Sunday" exposure to the Bible as a kid in rural Iowa. When I was a freshman at Iowa State University, two fellow students shared Christ with me one Saturday afternoon in early December in my dormitory room. I liked everything they had to say except Ephesians 2:8-9: "For it is by grace you have been saved, through faith . . . not by works" (NIV). I thought my Sunday school attendance pins would at least get me a little way toward heaven. Nevertheless, from December through April I participated in a beginners Bible study and attended a couple of Christian meetings. I was impressed—the skits were actually funny; not the typical religious stuff I expected.

All this culminated in my receiving Christ in May of the following year—six months later. It took that long to convince me I needed more than Sunday school attendance pins. If I had been pressed to pray the "sinner's prayer" that first Saturday afternoon in December, I wouldn't have wanted anything more to do with "Christians." In hindsight, I see that the slowly developed friendships with the college believers, the beginners Bible studies, the occasional radio sermons, and the years of church attendance were all part of a *process.*

The *link in the chain* diagram below helps me escape from feeling I must "reap" each time I share. It also frees me not to manipulate a conversation toward Christ. My desire is to reap when the time is right, but most of the time I hope to move a nonbeliever on to the next link. I am less concerned now with who does the reaping or when it happens and more interested in being a positive link myself.

The process of evangelism is also seen in Jesus' late-night chat with Nicodemus. In John 3:5, Jesus startled Nicodemus by saying, "Unless one is born of water and the Spirit he cannot enter into the kingdom of God." The analogy ("born of water") is physical birth. The birth of a baby is an *event* lasting from a few minutes up to many hours. But the event of physical birth is preceded by a nine-month *process* of gestation, followed by a twenty-year *process* of physical growth. So it is a *process* (gestation) followed by an *event* (birth) followed by a *process* (maturation). Similarly, spiritual birth is a *process* (sowing, watering, cultivating) followed by an *event* (conversion) followed by a *process* (discipleship).

Evangelism As a Process

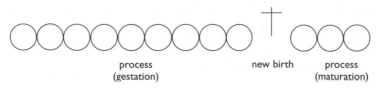

process   new birth   process
(gestation)   (maturation)

29

As you associate with nonbelievers, remember to relax. It doesn't all depend on you! You are on a big team—the body of Christ. Your teammates will back you up! Your link may not be the one where the prayer of repentance is prayed, but that link is possible only if others precede it. Your link is essential.

Another reason we must think of ourselves as links in a chain is that in today's culture fewer and fewer people (including Americans) share our biblical assumptions. They may not know about David, Goliath, or the apostle Paul. And who knows what they think about Jesus?

Notice the word "understand" in Matthew 13:19: "When anyone hears the word of the kingdom and does not *understand* it, the evil one comes and snatches away what has been sown in his heart. This is the one on whom seed was sown beside the road" (emphasis added).

Similarly, in Matthew 13:23 the word appears again: "And the one on whom seed was sown on the good soil, this is the man who hears the word and *understands* it" (emphasis added). Since not everyone has a Bible background, we have a responsibility to help our friends understand the gospel both intellectually and emotionally.

I was returning from a ministry planning meeting in the Rocky Mountains and decided to stop in Denver at a new restaurant where they serve soft drinks in tall, heavy glasses the size of orange highway safety cones. I brought my journal and a file folder into the restaurant to jot some notes and pray through some of the difficult issues from the meeting while they were still fresh. The restaurant was not busy, and the young waiter hung around my table watching me write while I sipped a 256-ounce Diet Coke.

"Are you writing a book?" he asked.

Fortunately, I had the presence of mind to sense God's leading, so I decided to take a chance. "No, I'm not a professional writer," I replied, "but I write about my spiritual journey, and sometimes my prayers."

"Really!" he responded. "That's interesting."

"Have you heard of that before?"

"No . . . never."

"Pull up a chair," I offered. "Doesn't look like you're too busy."

So my new waiter friend eagerly pulled up beside me and we talked about his exodus from California to Colorado and the Lutheran (he thought) uncle he was staying with. Then we returned to the subject of writing prayers. Easter had just passed, so I asked if he had heard of Jesus Christ.

"Sure!" he said. "Lots of times."

Realizing he might have to attend to other customers, I wanted to leave him with food for thought. So I ventured, "Have you heard of the resurrection of Jesus Christ?"

"Resurrection of Christ. What's that?"

I have talked with many secularized people, and I know I shouldn't be shocked by their lack of biblical knowledge. But I was alarmed that evening in Denver when I discovered that someone can live in America twenty years and not know about the resurrection of Christ. The young waiter was not ready to receive Christ; he needed *understanding,* and I was the next link in his chain. Before leaving, I got his card and later sent him a Bible with a letter of thanks for being such a gracious host.

My point? Not all your acquaintances are "ready to receive." Be part of the process of their coming to Christ. Be a link. Be sensitive to where they are, and seek to bring understanding.

Your Strategy Comes from the Saints, Not the Apostles

Shortly after we moved to Colorado Springs, a neighbor came striding across the street to welcome us. When he discovered I was with The Navigators, he said he too was a believer, but immediately confessed that he hadn't done much witnessing in the neighborhood and felt bad about

31

it. There I was in the middle of my driveway hearing a confession from a stranger! He went on. With another Christian next door, he said, "we" should launch a door-to-door campaign to share the gospel with everyone in the subdivision. "We," he said. Did I want to be part of that? Hmmm. Maybe not.

Why did I hesitate to jump on my well-meaning neighbor's ministry plan? Mormons and Jehovah's Witnesses come through at least once a year—what's wrong with Christians doing the same?

At the risk of sounding like an evangelical wimp, I have concluded that the apostolic model of aggressive, highly visible program preaching is not the norm for most believers. Yes, we must emulate Peter's zeal! Yes, we must follow Paul's willingness to endure suffering! Yes, we must be available to preach anywhere, just as Philip was! We must follow the apostles in *commitment,* but use different tactics. Why? Because we're not committed enough to go door to door? No—I am not ashamed of the gospel, and I don't think you are either. It's something else.

I have long been puzzled by the silence of the epistles on the subject of evangelism. With the foundation of the Great Commission given by Jesus in Matthew 28, wouldn't it be logical for the apostles to strongly exhort Jesus' followers to "get out and preach"?

Let's go back in time two thousand years to Ephesus. Imagine that you are a Greek shopkeeper raised in this exciting cosmopolitan city when Paul and his entourage arrive preaching Jesus. You are impressed by Paul's scholarly arguments, his debate in the synagogues, and his skill in reasoning with the lawyers. After hearing about Jesus and the resurrection, you realize that the Greek mythological gods mean nothing to you. And you can't help but notice how Paul's band of believers love one another.

Next you hear from a few Ephesian businessmen who claim to have found peace and joy from believing in Paul's message. Surprisingly, they have abandoned their mistresses and have begun treating their wives better. They even discarded their silver statues of the local goddess, Artemis.

Soon you, too, trust Christ, as do a few of your family members, and for two years you learn from Paul and the apostles at the School of Tyrannus. It's exciting. You have spoken tentatively to family and friends about Jesus. Deep in your soul you know this is the answer for your fellow Greeks, who are locked into a hedonistic search for meaning through mythology. They need to understand about Jesus—but how? If only Paul could preach to everyone!

Then yesterday, chaos! The silversmiths were so angered by Paul's preaching that they launched a riot. For two hours in the town square they shouted, "Great is Artemis of the Ephesians!" The silversmith guild was afraid that if Paul kept preaching people would no longer buy their idols of Artemis. Paul's life appeared to be in danger (complete story in Acts 19).

But today, a surprise! Paul announced that he and his companions are leaving for Macedonia immediately. You and your friends tearfully bid farewell to the entourage—probably never to see them again. Paul assures you he will write.

As you wave goodbye you whisper to your cousin Gaius, "Are *you* going to preach to the silversmiths? Who will debate in the synagogue with the Jewish scholars?"

"Not me," says Gaius. "I'm not a preacher like Paul."

"Perhaps your uncle Demetrius. He's outgoing. Can he quote from Isaiah?"

So, we arrive at this question: Are the saints of two years expected to duplicate Paul's ministry strategy? Should they preach in the same apostolic manner? I believe there is a different model for ministry for "non-apostles" like you and me—the insider model. Let's compare:

Do you see the difference? The apostles' "outside-in" strategy established a beachhead, whereas the strategy of the residents was to spread the gospel throughout the culture using natural webs of relationships.

Apostolic Model	Insider Model
• Coming in from outside (usually mobile)	• Residents already in place
• Highly intense preaching	• Sharing while living among them
• Supported by financial gifts usually	• Supported by earning their living
• Usually lightning rods for trouble	• Usually not lightning rods
• Intense preaching to crowds	• Sharing privately with individuals
• Short-duration ministry	• Long-duration ministry
• Highly committed to Christ	• Highly committed to Christ
• Zeal for the gospel (Colossians 4:3)	• Zeal for the gospel (Colossians 4:5-6)

Notice that both apostles and residents are expected to have zeal for the gospel. Paul did not expect his converts to be any less committed than he was. But I don't believe he expected them to copy his ministry tactics. Otherwise, why didn't he say so?

Mike Shamy of The Navigators pointed out to me that Colossians 4 gives insight into both the apostolic and the resident strategies: "Praying at the same time for us as well, that God may open up to us a door for the word, so that we may speak forth the mystery of Christ" (Colossians 4:3). Here Paul is asking for an open door to preach.

But contrast that with his exhortation to the Colossian believers in the next two verses: "Conduct yourselves with wisdom toward outsiders, making the most of the opportunity. Let your speech always be with grace, seasoned, as it were, with salt, so that you may know how you should respond to each person" (Colossians 4:5-6). The Colossians are already on the "inside" and don't need to ask for "open doors"; instead, they need wisdom in how they act with nonbelievers.

As you read the New Testament the differences in the two strategies become apparent. Here are two examples:

Admonitions from the epistles to preach publicly are infrequent at best. We must imitate Paul's zeal for the

Apostolic	Insider
• Acts 13:1-5: The church sends out Paul and Barnabas to evangelize other cities.	• 1 Thessalonians 1:8: The new believers at Thessalonica built a reputation for their faith—but never left Macedonia.
• Romans 1:1-5: Paul is called as an apostle.	• Romans 1:6-7: Roman Christians are called as saints.

gospel, but it would be incongruous to copy his unique methods.

But there's another factor: Paul's aggressive preaching was infectious. Not sharing modern apathetic tendencies, the resident converts didn't need Paul's exhortation to talk about Jesus—they couldn't keep their mouths shut about Him. In 1 Thessalonians 1:8, Paul commends the new believers at Thessalonica: "For the word of the Lord has sounded forth from you, not only in Macedonia and Achaia, but also in every place your faith toward God has gone forth, so that we have no need to say anything." The atmosphere was electric with natural evangelism, friend to friend, family to family—they couldn't keep quiet! Theologian Michael Green said it this way:

> The great mission of Christianity was in reality accomplished by means of informal missionaries . . . chattering to friends and chance acquaintances in homes and wine shops, on walks, and around market stalls. They went everywhere gossiping the gospel; they did it naturally . . . and with the conviction of those who are not paid to say that sort of thing.[1]

So if the saints were not to emulate the tactics of the apostles, what tactics did Paul exhort his converts to use? That's coming up next. But for now, realize that your models for ministry zeal are the apostles. But your models for ministry tactics are the saints—the insiders! Be who God made you to be.

CHAPTER FOUR

Stage One (Continued): Seven Guidelines for Reaching Nonbelievers

KEEPING IN MIND THAT EVANGELISM IS A PROCESS AND that the saints are our models, here are seven specific scriptural guidelines for relating to nonbelievers that we all can follow, regardless of our gifting.

1. Associate with Nonbelievers

An often-overlooked passage, 1 Corinthians 5:9-11, stands in contrast to the well-known teaching, "Be separate from the world." Here Paul corrects the Corinthians for being *too* separate:

> I wrote you in my letter not to associate with immoral people; I did not at all mean with the immoral people of this world, or with the covetous and swindlers, or with idolaters, for then you would have to go out of the world. But actually, I wrote to you not to associate with any so-called brother if he is an immoral person.

Paul reminds us not to abandon nonbelieving friends— otherwise we would have to leave the planet (go out of the world)! The ones we are to disassociate with are the so-called *believers* who are immoral. The Greek word translated "associate" is *sunanamignumi. Sunana* means "with" or "up," and *mignumi* means "to mingle."

This exhortation is the opposite of much evangelical thinking today, which advocates avoiding nonbelievers for fear of being corrupted. Unfortunately, though we avoid immoral pagans, we accommodate immoral "Christians" who do the same stuff. What message does this send to the watching world?

What about Jesus? Did he "mingle" with nonbelievers? Luke 15:2 reports that the Pharisees grumbled at Jesus, saying, "This man receives sinners and eats with them." And in Mark 2:15-17 Jesus is criticized for eating and drinking with tax collectors and sinners. Jesus responds, "It is not those who are healthy who need a physician, but those who are sick; I did not come to call the righteous, but sinners." Jesus had a reputation for hanging out with the unconverted! By contrast, many dedicated believers today hang out mostly with the converted. They do not have genuine friendships with nonbelievers, even though they associate with them daily on the job or in their neighborhoods.

A few years ago I was teaching a Sunday school class of young marrieds on the subject of evangelism. These were some of the sharpest people in the church—launching promising careers, socially in tune, the kind of people upon whom strong churches are built. After a couple weeks of laying the biblical groundwork, I passed out index cards and posed this assignment:

> Think of the nonbelievers in your world—at work, in the neighborhood, at the health club, and so on. List the names of those you could invite to your home for a meal on a Friday or Saturday night in the next few weeks. Your goal is not to spring the gospel on them, but just to enjoy a nice evening together.

Silence. They just stared at me. I repeated the question. They studied the index cards intently, as if hoping names would magically appear from the cotton fibers of the paper. Slowly, a few picked up their pens and doodled on the cards. But most did nothing. Embarrassed, I ventured, "Is this a difficult question?"

A class member finally broke the silence. "Scott, we have nonChristian acquaintances, but we don't have nonChristian friends. And especially none we want in our homes."

"But you work with nonbelievers every day; you're around them all the time!" I countered.

He went on, "But they're not our friends. We don't know them well. And besides, what if they cussed or smoked in our homes? They make us nervous."

The other class members nodded in agreement. One by one they revealed their reticence to engage nonbelievers in friendship. They were more comfortable entertaining Christian friends, hiring Christian plumbers, going to Christian hairdressers, and patronizing Christian restaurants. I was shocked. But I shouldn't have been. I have discovered that Christians hanging out with Christians is the norm. Befriending nonbelievers is unusual. We believers have become our own ghetto with our own language, our own manners, and our own plumbers! It's more comfortable that way.

In some cities you can find directories of Christian businesses. Believers wish for Christian bosses at work and sacrifice financially to send their kids to Christian schools. The message? Insulate yourselves from nonbelieving plumbers, agnostic hairdressers, and evil teachers in the public schools. So deeply entrenched is this unspoken value that when a young couple in our Bible study group discovered "Christian neighbors" at their new house, they were grateful that God had "blessed" them. But shouldn't we be asking God to put us beside nonbelieving neighbors?

Martin Marty, theologian and editor of *Context*, says that two main cultures exist side by side in America — evangelicals and everybody else. He says both are "so separate that neither acts as if the other exists."

But isolation is not difficult to resolve. Start by deciding to intentionally hang out with nonbelievers. Why not list half a dozen nonbelievers to pray for, asking God to give you opportunities to get to know them? Maybe you'll like them!

Second, initiate outings. The old adage is true: "The one who would have friends must prove to be friendly." Though we are not consistent, my wife Alma and I purposely initiate a friendship-building activity with nonbelievers once a week, in addition to incidental contact. So rather than hang out with our Christian friends, we invite nonbelieving friends to popular restaurants, to our home, or to the theater.

Do we share the gospel on these occasions? Usually not. Springing out a hidden agenda is like rolling a hand grenade onto the coffee table. I've done that! It's not pretty, and your friends will not respond to your next invitation for a "fun evening out." But neither do we hide our faith; Alma and I share all aspects of our lives.

Even if you don't share the gospel, initiating an evening with nonbelieving friends is something Jesus would do. Remember, you are a link in the chain, and the "sweet aroma of the knowledge of Him" seeps out through you (2 Corinthians 2:14). Just be close enough that they can smell it! And relax—enjoy the people God has brought into your world. He will tip you off when it is time to share the gospel.

One caution: if you are a new believer recovering from an addiction (like alcohol), please be careful. The nonbelievers you hang out with can pull you back into old habits. I once mentored a new believer who confessed, "Scott, when I go to the grocery store the beer aisle still calls my name." His brothers and sisters are heavy drinkers, and when he is with them he is tempted to go back to drunkenness. Limiting his contact with them is his only option for now.

2. Don't Force New Believers to Switch Cultures at Conversion

When I was in collegiate ministry, our group was primarily Protestant, but soon some nonpracticing Catholic friends came to know Christ. We were delighted, but some "mature" students and a pastor or two around town wanted me to insist that the Catholic students attend a "Bible church." After all, they needed "good doctrine."

Fortunately, the Lord guided me to 1 Corinthians 7:20 and 24. Paul was addressing a controversial issue: should non-Jewish converts to Christ be circumcised? Paul's answer: "Each one should remain in the situation which he was in when God called him" (verse 20).

In other words, if God called you as a Gentile, stay Gentile. Accordingly, I recommended that the Catholic believers stay "Catholic," that our Presbyterian believers stay "Presbyterian," and so on. Yanking a Catholic or a Lutheran or a Presbyterian to a "Bible church" is not merely a change of Sunday morning activity, but a change in culture.

Similarly, in overseas ministry, when Muslim converts drop the mosque in favor of a "Western" church they are ostracized. The Western missionaries become their only friends, and ministering back to their culture is impossible. This is one reason the church has had so little impact in some nonChristian cultures.

When you lead people to Christ, don't yank them out of their religious and cultural heritage and drag them to yours. Let them stay in the condition in which they were called, and help them live for Christ there. Maybe that is why Jesus told those He healed to go back to their homes and tell the mighty works of God (Mark 5:19).

3. Develop Credibility with Nonbelievers

A few years ago I made a mistake on this one. I had been asked by the Audubon Society to lead a bird-watching hike of Glen Eyrie canyon, the home of The Navigators and a good spot for birds. About twenty-five of us gathered one cool May morning at 7 A.M. I fell into step with "George" (not his real name) and his wife, explaining the history of Glen Eyrie as we slowly walked the canyon, pausing now and then to gaze through binoculars. They enjoyed the three-hour hike immensely and thanked me profusely. We even exchanged phone numbers.

A few weeks later I was starting a Friday morning "skeptics' Bible study," so I called bird-watcher George and invited him to lunch. We met at Mollica's, a little Italian place near his office, and we quickly picked up our friendship from the bird outing. But the conversation cooled noticeably when I invited him to the Bible group. He was polite, but a tenseness came over him as we finished our meal. Nevertheless, he came to the first study! It was a cordial study with plenty of doughnuts, a little laughter, and a discussion on John 1 with ten newcomers, mostly unbelievers. But George never came again. And he never returned my phone calls. End of story.

What went wrong? I could say, "Well, he was convicted of sin—another secularist running from God." Maybe. Or was he scared off by my aggressive tactics? Going back to the link in the chain diagram, it is likely that George was nowhere near understanding the gospel. Or perhaps he or his wife had a previous bad experience with religion. I wish I had built the friendship more before I invited him to the study. I applaud my boldness, but I deplore my lack of wisdom.

What do the apostles advise? I like the way Peter says it: "Live such good lives among the pagans that, though they accuse you of doing wrong, they may see your good deeds and glorify God on the day he visits us" (1 Peter 2:12, NIV). And Paul adds: "Make it your ambition to lead a quiet life and attend to your own business and work with your hands, just as we commanded you; so that you will behave properly toward outsiders and not be in any need" (1 Thessalonians 4:11-12).

If the gospel has made no difference in our lives and if we are not attractive to nonbelievers, then our words about Christ are to no avail. It's like the bumper sticker: *I believe in you, God, but save me from your followers!*

An older gentleman from a small town in the Midwest told Alma and me that even though he grew up in the church, he refused to come to Christ in his youth. He said, "Church people were the main reason I didn't want anything to do with God."

"Why not? Didn't you gain something from going to church?" I responded.

"Yes, I got a Bible background, but my mind was set against God the day me and my buddies came to the Sunday morning service with work clothes on. The church members sneered at us. One woman even said we should not go into God's house dressed like that. But those were Depression days and that was all we had." He never went back to church until thirty years later, when a Christ-centered friend burst his stereotype and won him to the Lord.

You probably have friends who have told you they are not believers because of "those hypocritical Christians." We might argue that the nonbelievers are hiding behind the hypocrite issue. That may be true, but they are not likely to be argued out from behind it. God may be speaking to them, but it is our role to get close enough to them to win credibility for the gospel. Although we need not be perfect, we must be genuine!

4. Life Witness Is Not Enough — You Must Speak

Here is a danger. Some Christians, hearing that building credibility for the gospel is absolutely crucial, revert to the old escapism: "I witness by life—not by lip." Armed with a biblical excuse to witness only by life, they go to the extreme and say nothing. They become like the Yukon River in Alaska—frozen at the mouth! Accompanying this mindset is a saying attributed to Saint Francis of Assisi: "Share the gospel, and if necessary, use words." Who could disagree? Without credibility, we will not be taken seriously. But are we never to speak? I asked author and missionary statesman LeRoy Eims about Saint Francis's statement. He replied wisely, "Scott, words will be necessary! How many come to Christ without the words of the gospel being shared sooner or later?"

Granted, some people find God without a human witness, but most read the good news in the Bible, or hear it from a friend or on the radio or at church. We cannot discount the necessity to verbalize the gospel. Genuine friendship implies that we will share what is most precious to us just as we expect our friends to share what is precious to them. At a certain point, Jesus will come up in the conversation, and they will listen gladly.

A few years ago some believers in Minneapolis banded together to pray and encourage one another to reach their nonbelieving friends. They knew they could do more together than they could on their own. They did many things right: they hung out with nonbelievers; they introduced their friends to other believers; they were genuine. They even went on camping trips together, where it is impossible not to be vulnerable. They built tremendous credibility for the gospel. But after three years none of their friends were close to coming to Christ.

In reviewing their progress (or lack of it) for advancing the gospel they concluded: "We've drunk a lot of beer with nonbelievers, and we've eaten a lot of potato chips, but we haven't shared the gospel." Of course, bits and pieces of the gospel had been shared over three years, but they had not developed sustained times of reading the Scriptures with their friends.

Why bring the Scriptures into it? Simple. Power! Once nonbelievers engage honestly with the words of Jesus, they will be hooked. There is nothing you can say or do that is a more powerful witness than the words of Jesus Himself. Romans 1:16 says, "For I am not ashamed of the gospel, for it is the *power* of God for salvation" (emphasis added). By the way, I no longer use the term "Bible study," because to some nonbelievers the word "study" is too threatening or carries bad baggage. I simply invite them to read the Bible with me.

Believers who solemnize the "life but not lips" idea don't understand Philippians 2:14-16, which reminds us to live godly lives in the midst of a "crooked and depraved generation, in which you shine like stars in the universe *as you hold out the word of life*" (verse 16, NIV, emphasis added). Do you see it? As you hold out the word of life! Credibility is not an end in itself.

The Holy Spirit will prompt you when it is time to invite your nonbelieving friends to read the Bible with you. Don't do it too soon like I did with bird-watcher George! But don't wait too long, either. You might run out of potato chips.

5. Share the Gospel, Not the Baggage

In your exuberance to talk about Jesus, you might be tempted to also share your convictions about attending church, stopping abortion, getting pornography off television, allowing prayer before football games, and voting Republican. I call this "gospel creep." Unfortunately, listeners assume that a follower of Jesus must buy the whole package — that they must become like you to follow Christ. They equate the message with the messenger.

Paul, the learned Pharisee, probably had strong opinions about the social issues of Corinth, but in 1 Corinthians 2:2 he says, "For I determined to know nothing among you except Jesus Christ, and Him crucified." Paul could have focused on the evils of injustice in the Roman system or the excesses of the emperors. Instead, he focused on Christ.

Maybe praying before a football game is OK, but that is not the gospel. That is not why Jesus went to the cross. Let a new follower decide those issues for herself. As new believers walk with Christ, He will speak to them about social issues. Your role: preach Jesus and nothing else. Missionary statesman E. Stanley Jones, who served in India, said:

I once traveled, during my formative evangelistic years, with a very great man. When he was on Christ he was the most effective man I knew. But when his emphasis shifted from Christ to varying emphases — anti-war programs, social justice, birth control, spiritualism — he was less than effective; he was a blur.[1]

Let's not be a blur! Jesus alone! Keep your theme on following Him.

6. Be Different, but Flexible

In my early days as a believer, I suspected that those who advocated making friends with nonbelievers just wanted a justification for drinking beer — big sins by my youthful Iowa evangelical standards. Didn't Paul clearly teach in 2 Corinthians 6:14 that believers are to be different? "Do not be bound together [unequally yoked] with unbelievers; for what partnership have righteousness and lawlessness, or what fellowship has light with darkness?"

But in 1 Corinthians 9:19-23 Paul says he has made himself a slave to both Jews and Gentiles in order to win them. For example, in 9:22 he writes: "To the weak I became weak, that I might win the weak; I have become all things to all men, that I may by all means save some."

Does this imply that we are to behave like nonbelievers to win them to Christ? Let's look more closely at 1 Corinthians 10. Some new believers in Paul's day considered it wrong to eat meat that had been used in pagan idolatry rituals. So before purchasing meat in the marketplace or eating at a friend's house they would ask, "Has this meat been offered to idols?" Could be awkward at a black tie dinner party!

Paul encouraged the Corinthians to go ahead and eat without asking questions, for the sake of the nonbelieving host. This is an example of becoming all things to all people. It does not mean adopting their values, but it does mean bending your social convictions where biblical absolutes are not at stake. You flex to accommodate others. Don't ask them to accommodate you.

A personal example of being flexible occurred on a family vacation to Door County, Wisconsin. My five-year-old son, Andrew, and I were walking down a secluded dirt road near our rented cabin. It was a warm day in March, but the ice pack was still on Green Bay. As we walked by an old run-down house the owner hailed us. We stopped to talk in the driveway. He was wrinkled, with a scanty lineup of brownish front teeth. Unshaven, smelly, and dressed in work clothes, he seemed glad to be outdoors after a long Wisconsin winter.

We chatted politely for a few minutes, but Andrew and I wanted to get back to exploring the road. Then the old man told us his wife had died the year before and he was lonely. We listened. We empathized. Then he invited us into the house to show us her picture. I hesitated, but I thought this might be a divine appointment.

The house was a mess; grotesque stacks of stuff were piled on the kitchen table. It was obvious the Mrs. had been gone for a while. Then his face lit up as he told us of the homemade brew that he and his wife made every year. Would we like to sample it?

Beer! A drinking party with my innocent five-year-old son on Green Bay? Andrew's eyes were as big as Heineken bottle caps. At the precious age of five he already knew it was a sin to drink beer, wine, and whiskey, and he wasn't too sure about root beer. I glanced down to him. A sly smile crossed his face, as if to say, "I won't tell Mom if you won't." I felt uncomfortable, but the old man was beaming expectantly.

"Sure! I'd love to sample some of your brew." So we stayed another twenty minutes and heard more about his beloved departed wife. I was able to share the love of Christ with him in a natural way, and he appreciated it. Though we never saw him again, I'm glad I was able to "be all things to all men" that day.

What happened here? I flexed my convictions on a

nonissue to accommodate a hurting widower for an hour on Green Bay. I was a link in the chain for the love of Christ. Would I have won a hearing for the gospel if I had lectured him on the evils of alcohol? The point is this: *Be different!* You must! Romans 12:2 exhorts us strongly, "Do not be conformed to this world." But also, *be flexible!* Unless biblical absolutes are involved, don't make unbelievers uncomfortable by demanding that they move to your position. You be the one who is uncomfortable. And why? To "win the more" for the "sake of the gospel."

Caution: sometimes believers try too hard to be all things to all people and forget to be genuine. Virgil, a Christian friend and a nondrinker, decided to buy a six-pack to win the heart of his beer-drinking neighbor. Though Virgil had never darkened the door of a liquor store even in his nonChristian days, he ventured out and bought some beer. The next day he hollered across the fence to his neighbor to come over for a cold one.

"No thanks," the neighbor said. "I quit." Laughing about it later, Virgil told me he kept that six-pack in his refrigerator for months as a reminder of how over-eager he was to be flexible.

7. Be Ready to Share Clearly

Suppose a nonbelieving friend asked you how to become a Christian. What would you say? Or suppose you were asked why a loving and sovereign God allows evil in the world. Or what about the issue of wars—weren't most wars fought over differences in religion? Can you accurately and wisely respond to these issues?

Not knowing how to wisely respond often leads evangelicals to theological arguments with their nonbelieving friends, and they end up with strained relationships. Peter exhorts us on this issue in 1 Peter 3:15-16 (NIV): "Always be prepared to give an answer to everyone who asks you to give the reason for the hope that you have. But do this with gentleness and respect, keeping a clear conscience, so that those who speak maliciously against your good behavior in Christ may be ashamed of their slander."

"Be prepared!" That will require homework. Too often we evangelicals use a different verse for sharing our faith—Mark 13:11 (NIV): "Whenever you are arrested and brought to trial, do not worry beforehand about what to say. Just say whatever is given you at the time, for it is not you speaking but the Holy Spirit."

True, we must rely on the Holy Spirit, but the Mark 13 passage refers to the end times, when we are brought before authorities. Also, it doesn't prohibit preparation! It simply tells us *not to worry* about what we will say. Are we using the "whatever is given you at the time" mantra as an excuse?

The first thing to be prepared for is sharing the gospel. Can you make the good news clear in a few minutes without weighing it down with extraneous baggage? If I'm in a pinch at a restaurant, I write out John 3:16 on a napkin and walk through it, defining key words and phrases. Or, if I have more time, I draw out the bridge illustration. (See page 152 for an example.)

We must not ignore nonbelievers' honest questions. It shows disrespect to assume they want to dodge the issue of Christ and reply, "That is an irrelevant question; the real issue is about Jesus . . . now, as I was saying. . . ." Here are some questions I have been asked that I wish I had been better prepared to address:

- Religious wars have caused more deaths than any other factor. Why is that so? (Actually, godless Hitler and Stalin were responsible for more deaths than all the "religious wars" combined.)
- Why does a good and sovereign God allow so much human suffering?
- The Bible is a collection of fables—how can it be trusted? How can a man be swallowed by a whale (great fish, actually) and live through it?

- If Christ is the only way (as you tell me), what about those who have never heard of Him? Are they doomed?

Thick books have been written on these subjects. The hard part is condensing the answers to bite-size portions that meet the needs of the questioners. I suggest you do your own research and come up with answers appropriate for your listeners. Prepare!

The apostle Peter reminds us to answer questions with gentleness, respect, and a clear conscience. It is easy to be sucker-punched into an argument when our questioners push our sacred buttons — we defend the faith with the zeal of Martin Luther at Worms. I enjoy the profound answers a particular radio preacher gives in defense of the faith, but I don't like his attitude. I don't want to be like him, even though he seems brilliant. Nonbelievers may feel the same about us. If you don't know an answer, simply say, "I don't know. I'm puzzled about that too."

Finally, note the phrase "to everyone who asks you to give the reason for the hope that you have" (1 Peter 3:15). Today many nonbelievers are not attracted to the lives of believers, so they are not asking questions. They see no "hope" that whets their appetite to know God. That should get our attention. Are we evangelicals living lives that "demand an explanation?" Keep in mind that nonbelievers will not ask, "Can you give me a reason for the hope that is in you?" Their questions or comments will be more indirect, such as:

- Your kids seem well behaved.
- You mentioned a Sunday class you attend. What's it like?
- Where do you go to church?
- You always seem so happy.

Evangelism is more art than science, more a dance than a formula. Living out these seven exhortations from the apostles does not guarantee you'll win nonbelievers to Christ. Fruitfulness in evangelism is determined by God's work in the hearts of nonbelievers. Stay close to the vine, do as the apostles exhort, and leave the results to God. Faithfulness is your target. And remember to live in close enough proximity to your nonbelieving friends for them to notice.

Now, as God gives you new believers, or as you "adopt" Christians who want to grow spiritually, how do you disciple them to maturity?

CHAPTER FIVE

Stage Two: Discipling from the Heart

MANY CHURCHES AND MINISTRIES STOP AFTER EVANGELISM. They don't intend to stop, but they make false assumptions like:

- Converts will become involved in a fellowship.
- Converts will naturally grow in Christ.
- Converts know the how-tos of spiritual disciplines.

Also, it is sometimes assumed that new believers are ready to serve in the church, so they are immediately voted into usher, deacon, and Sunday school teacher roles. But do they have the necessary biblical grounding?

It's time for a reality check: How many new believers become vibrant, dedicated disciples of Christ with changed lives? And how many become effective in reaching others? We are thrilled to see throngs coming in the front doors of our churches and ministries. But who's watching the back doors? Twelve-week discipleship programs alone cannot stop the exodus of disillusioned, tired converts.

Everyone knows discipleship is needed, but unfortunately, it is more often talked about than effectively done. Listen to this comment from Jim Petersen, veteran missionary to Brazil:

If you have been around the Christian community at all, you know about discipleship. It is there on the right-hand side of the page of the church bulletin. The discipleship group meets Tuesday for breakfast at Underwood's Restaurant. In our bigger churches, we have pastors of discipleship. Our Christian bookstores always have a section reserved for discipleship materials. There you will find everything from a study booklet for new believers to complete courses in discipleship. Many of us have taken the course.[1]

Realizing there is more to discipling others than a Wednesday night class, let's analyze the second stage of our process—discipling. Remember, the stages are not distinct; they run together.

Discipling is a lifelong process, but the first step is *follow up*. Identifying where the term *follow up* came from will give us a good start in understanding its importance. Let's learn a lesson from history featuring Billy Graham and Dawson Trotman, founder of The Navigators.

Dawson Trotman came to Christ in 1926 through memorizing Scripture and soon became an aggressive personal evangelist. What Billy Graham did with large crowds, Dawson did one to one with sailors during World War II. "Winning souls" was strongly urged on evangelicals in those days, and Dawson won many.

Stages of Personal Ministry

Compassionate Laborers

New Believers

Growing Disciples

One hot day in Southern California in 1940, Dawson picked up a hitchhiker along a dusty road. As the hitchhiker got into the car he muttered, "Jesus Christ, it's hot out there today." Dawson winced as he heard the name of his Savior taken in vain, so he gave the young man a gospel tract, saying, "Here, lad, read this." And soon Dawson led this unsuspecting hitchhiker in a heartfelt prayer to receive Christ.

One year later Dawson was driving down the same hot, dusty road, saw a hitchhiker, and offered him a ride. As the hitchhiker got into the car he muttered, "Jesus Christ, it's hot out there today!" Again, Dawson winced, so he proceeded to share the gospel. The hitchhiker said, "Don't I know you?" It was the same hitchhiker from the year before.

Dawson was shocked! His assumption that new believers would naturally grow spiritually, just as he had, was wrong. So he began to concentrate on following up—helping converts get established in Christ. It was no longer enough to lead someone to faith. These new "babes in Christ" needed help in spiritual growth in the same way that human babies need help in physical growth.

So Dawson and The Navigators developed Bible studies, Scripture memory packets, and seminars to help converts grow. And it worked! By the time Pearl Harbor was attacked, there were "Navigator sailors" on over a thousand ships of the Pacific fleet.

In the 1950s, Billy Graham came to Dawson and explained that in the great revivals of history, there was never much of a "follow up program" to help new believers grow. He asked for Dawson's help. But Dawson told Billy he was too busy working with sailors and launching The Navigators. "You'll have to get someone else," he said.

Before the words were out of Dawson's mouth, the 6'2" Graham grabbed the 5'6" Trotman by the shoulders and said, "Who else? Who's been majoring in this?"

It was true that Dawson and The Navigators had been majoring in follow up. So Trotman and some of his meager staff worked with the Graham organization from 1949 to 1954, pioneering the follow up methods and materials still used by the Graham team. Now, fifty years later, the term *follow up* is common among Christian leaders, though it has given way to another, more comprehensive term: *discipling.*

Think of it this way: my daughter and son-in-law recently had a baby. They brought little Laura home from the hospital to a room in their home equipped with a crib, bassinet, diapers, towels, and all the things a new little life needs to grow.

Suppose they told her, "Little Laura, welcome to our home! We are delighted you have joined the family. In this home is everything you will need to grow—diapers in the top dresser drawer, milk in the refrigerator, blankets on the bed, books in the bookcase, and cosmetics in the dresser drawer for when you are older. There's even a subscription to *Babies Monthly.* And when you're ready for your teenage tattoo, here is the phone number of a medically approved tattoo artist. Let us know if you need anything else. We're available. We're on our way to the mall, and then to tennis lessons, but we'll be back soon. Take care!"

Just as it is unwise to expect a new baby to grow without parenting, so it is unwise to expect a young convert to grow spiritually without follow up. But I confess that I have too often treated new babes in Christ that way—"Call me if you need help!" Shameful.

But sometimes spiritual parents go to the opposite extreme of "hoovering" a new convert. Hoovering is what a vacuum cleaner does—hovering close above the carpet, rushing air through it, dominating the carpet's worldview. It works in cleaning carpets, but hoovering debilitates new believers. Give them freedom. Be careful of over-control. What is the balance?

In 1 Thessalonians are seven "heart" guidelines for spiritual parenting. These attitudes will not tell you *what* to share with a new believer, but they will guide you in how to *relate to* those you disciple. For ideas on teachings to give a new believer, check the chart on page 25, "Topics to Share Next."

1. An Interceding Heart

In 1 Thessalonians 1:2 Paul says, "We always thank God for all of you, mentioning you in our prayers" (NIV). The late Navigators missionary Warren Myers pointed out that much has been written about William Carey, the "father of modern missions," who served for decades in India two hundred years ago, "but nothing has been written about his bedridden, 'useless' sister," who prayed for Carey and his converts hour after hour from her bed. That sister had the heart of a discipler.

When you pray for new believers, you are in good company. John 17 records Jesus Christ's prayers for His disciples. Colossians 4:12 describes Epaphras as "always laboring earnestly for you in his prayers." Note the words *always* and *laboring*. Not once in a while, but *always*. And *laboring*—intercessory prayer is not dreamy reverie, but hard work. Epaphras loved people enough to work hard in prayer. He had the heart of a discipler.

There is nothing better you can do for new believers than to pray for them. What can you pray? Scripture is rich with patterns for intercession—from Jesus' John 17 prayer to the many prayers of Paul that are recorded in his epistles. Read Paul's letters—especially Ephesians, Philippians, and Colossians—and highlight his prayers for fellow believers. In time, his prayers will become yours.

2. An Initiating Heart

Paul didn't wait for the new believers in Thessalonica to ask for help—he initiated help! Note 1 Thessalonians 2:2 (NIV): "We dared to tell you his gospel in spite of strong opposition."

My daughter and son-in-law didn't wait for little Laura to invite them to "follow up." She came home from the hospital to a room freshly painted, a little bed already made, diapers, bottles, and burp cloths neatly arranged. Parents take initiative.

Yet with spiritual newborns, taking initiative requires taking risks. Your overtures to meet for Bible study could be rejected. You may feel like you are crowding into their busy lives, inconveniencing them. Take heart! Jesus crowded into a new believer's day. In John 9 He healed a blind man, who was then criticized by the Pharisees. They suspected a trick and even asked the man's parents if their son was truly born blind. Finally, they kicked him out of the synagogue. Imagine the newly healed man's confusion!

Verse 35 (NIV) says, "Jesus heard that they had thrown him out, and when he found him, he said, 'Do you believe in the Son of Man?'" *When He found him!* Jesus took initiative to find the man and follow up on his new faith. He didn't wait for the man to find Him.

I'm glad a grad student, Bob Van Zante, took initiative to mentor me, or I would not have grown in Christ— I didn't even know which questions to ask! Think about it: Most of us, as new believers, did not seek out a Bible study or a mentoring relationship with a spiritual coach. Someone else dared to make the first move. A discipler takes initiative.

3. A Motherly Heart

Paul says in 1 Thessalonians 2:7 (NIV), "We were gentle among you, like a mother caring for her little children." Spiritual babies, like other newborns, need gentleness. What does this motherly heart look like in a discipler?

It was time for my regular meeting with Adam, an eager new follower of Christ. I'd observed he had developed some pretty devastating patterns of communication with his wife. Boy, did I have a stiff spiritual pep talk ready for him! But as soon as we greeted each other, I knew something was wrong. So I spent the noon hour listening to him describe his hostile mother-in-law, who said to his new stepchildren, "You don't have to obey Adam; he's not your real father."

Adam was crushed. This was not the day for a pep talk. This was a day to be gentle. So I listened. I empathized. Part of the time we just sat silently. Then it was time to go. As he opened his car door outside Taco John's, he paused, hugged me, and told me he loved me.

Gentleness means listening rather than fixing, keeping silent rather than speaking, putting an arm on the shoulder rather than exhorting. Paul knew when to be gentle like a mother. Such is the heart of a discipler.

4. A Fatherly Heart

Not only was Paul as gentle as a mother, he also played the role of father by "exhorting and encouraging and imploring each one of you as a father would his own children" (1 Thessalonians 2:11).

At times you'll need to strongly exhort a new believer to take a bold step for which he feels unprepared. Sometimes you'll need to prepare the person you're helping to make it without you—just as a father prepares his child for independence. Sometimes your fathering role requires you to challenge another person to face up to a weakness or an obvious sin. It's daunting—and risky. But a father is willing to take the risk in order to see his children walk with maturity.

Back to Adam. I still needed to talk with him as a spiritual father about his incessant rambling in conversation. It was visibly devastating his wife, Joan, who had little chance to talk. He didn't realize that these rabbit-chasing, rambling soliloquies dishonored her. I hesitated to exhort as a father for fear of losing Adam's friendship. Couldn't I, too, be accused of rambling?

Finally, during one of our biweekly get-togethers at Margo's Hot Dog Stand, I gathered up courage and said, "Adam, I've got a suggestion." I told him courteously but frankly that he was violating a principle of good communication. And I gave examples of specific rabbits I'd seen him chase while Joan and others could only listen politely and check their watches. Silence. *Uh-oh,* I thought, *he's not taking this very well.* Finally, he smiled and thanked me. Then he asked how to overcome this bad habit.

At our next Bible study, he caught himself rambling, stopped, glanced at me, and smiled. Joan smiled, too, and started contributing. That day at the hot dog stand, a victory was won—not just with Adam, but with me. God gave me grace to be more intent on pleasing Him than on pleasing Adam. God is the third party in a discipling relationship. He was present with Paul in Thessalonica; He was present with me at Margo's; and He will be present with you, too. No one understands the father-heart of a discipler better than God.

Having the heart of a father doesn't always mean correcting. Sometimes it's a matter of encouraging or sharing a meaningful verse of Scripture. A good father considers the moment and asks, "What is most needed at this time?" A good father also realizes that children are different, so he deals with them individually.

5. An Open Heart

Paul told the Thessalonians he was "delighted to share with [them] not only the gospel of God but our lives as well" (2:8, NIV). New believers need more than information or even inspiration: they need incarnation. They must see how the gospel works in everyday life. Words alone won't do it!

How do you share your life with a new believer? Here are some suggestions.

Be vulnerable. Relate your struggles—not just your victories. People won't think less of you, but rather will be encouraged to know that you are normal. I still recall the time I saw a mature mentor chicken out of a clear witnessing opportunity. He admitted it. Though he was discouraged, I was elated! I no longer felt alone in my struggles.

Get together. Notice the phrase "among you" in 1 Thessalonians 1:5 and 2:7. Invite your protégé to accompany you to the dry cleaners where you were bilked on a ketchup-stained jacket. She needs to see you struggle to be gracious and realize that she, too, needs to control her feelings and words. Let people you disciple see you live your life. Don't limit your contact to once-a-week, hour-long, structured appointments.

Open your home. Bring new disciples into your house or apartment. Let them see that your stove needs cleaning and your garage is a mess, lest they get the idea they must be perfect in everything. Let them observe your family relationships—how you have devotions as a family, how you handle conflict with a spouse or roommate, and so on. They need to see that your relationship with Christ affects you on the home front.

All of this requires a great investment of time. It's the most valuable thing you can give new believers. Bring them into your day-to-day victories and struggles. Anyone can share a message; it takes the heart of a disciple to share one's personal life.

6. A Blameless Heart

Paul said the Thessalonians were witnesses as to how "holy, righteous and blameless we were among you who believed" (2:10, NIV). One aspect of blamelessness is represented in the old saying, "What you are speaks so loudly I can't hear what you say." There must be congruence between your message and your behavior. A friend once commented about a Christian leader, "I guess I respect him, but I don't want to become like him." Why not? Incongruence.

Here are other examples: You exhort your new believer to have a daily quiet time, but do you have a quiet time? You extol the value of memorizing Scripture, but do you memorize? You frown at others who watch R-rated movies, but do you watch them? It is hypocritical to lead where you are not modeling. Your protégé will see through it.

7. An Honest Heart

In 1 Thessalonians 2:3, Paul assures his friends of the sincerity of his motives. In verse 5 (NIV) he declares, "We never used flattery, nor did we put on a mask to cover up greed." In verses 4 and 6 he makes it clear that he is not seeking approval or praise from people; rather, he is seeking only to please God. Both Paul's motives and his methods were pure. His conduct was faultless. His discipler's heart was right with God and with people. It is so easy to pay insincere compliments in hopes that your mentorees will like you better. Don't do it.

When does discipling end? How do you know when you are done? Or does it, like physical parenting, go on forever? Below is the *wheel illustration* (see pages 148-149 on how to use the wheel in discipling.). This classic illustration was developed by Dawson Trotman and The Navigators to help sailors develop spiritual discipline. It began as a three-legged milking stool with the legs being the Word, prayer, and evangelism. But Dawson couldn't stomach the idea of a Christian sitting down on the job, so he changed it to a wheel. Though this wheel has been around since the 1940s, I still share it with those I'm discipling, and I have yet to find one person who is not

inspired by the simple concepts it presents. The wheel concepts give an attainable goal to aim toward. Actually, the illustration points to Christ as the focus and our obedience to Him. The four spokes are simply four disciplines each of us needs to master.

Christ certainly must be in the center of a believer's life. The vertical spokes of the Word and prayer show how God speaks to us and we to Him. And the natural outworking of our vertical relationship is how we relate to people—fellowship with believers and evangelism to nonbelievers. The four disciplines are never an end in themselves, but rather "habits" that enable us to transfer the power of Christ into a life of obedience. When the wheel is moving, the spokes are a blur—like the spokes of buckboard wagons in old Western movies. It is Christ, the center, who is seen by outsiders.

But is that all discipling is—mastering the spiritual disciplines? Of course not, but with these disciplines firmly in place, your "disciple" can feed himself with God. He can weather any storm. And he is not dependent on you!

CHAPTER SIX

Stage Three: Developing Compassionate Laborers

DOES PERSONAL MINISTRY STOP ONCE A BELIEVER "MASTERS" the spiritual disciplines? Is your work finished then?

Once, over lunch at a Holiday Inn, I was showing the *stages diagram* below to a Christian leader. I pointed to the wheel illustration and said, "We cannot stop with discipling a person; we must go on to equip him." Then I pointed to the equipping stage. But he abruptly stopped me. He said the equipping section is not needed because Jesus commanded us to "make disciples." Furthermore, he said that if a person was truly a disciple, he would also get involved in service. No need for equipping!

Stages of Personal Ministry

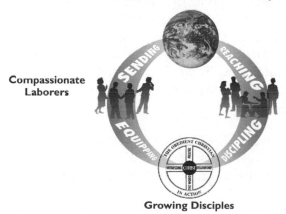

Compassionate Laborers

New Believers

Growing Disciples

Technically he is right—a true disciple will minister to others. But it has been my observation that too many "disciples" engage only in "corporate service"—not personal evangelism and discipling. They serve in their churches as ushers, deacons, elders, Sunday school superintendents, and nursery workers—often simultaneously! Corporate service is fine, but it is not enough.

Also, I've noticed that many Christian leaders do not know how to help growing disciples move beyond the basic disciplines summarized in the wheel. If disciples run into marriage problems or need counseling, pastors know how to help. But healthy disciples are usually neglected in favor of parishioners with urgent counseling issues.

This brings us to the need for *lifelong laborers* who can help these healthy disciples overcome normal problems and keep progressing in their walk with God. To develop lifelong laborers, we must begin by defining the word *laborer*. Once we know what a laborer looks like, we can guide a growing disciple toward becoming one.

Here is where I began years ago on our back porch in Madison, Wisconsin. Because I was experiencing only mediocre success in one-to-one mentoring, I decided to look again at Jesus' words in Matthew 9:35-38:

> Jesus was going about all the cities and villages, teaching in their synagogues, and proclaiming the gospel of the kingdom, and healing every kind of disease and every kind of sickness. And seeing the multitudes, He felt compassion for them, because they were distressed and downcast like sheep without a shepherd. Then He said to His disciples, "The harvest is plentiful, but the workers are few. Therefore beseech the Lord of the harvest to send out workers into His harvest."

From this passage we see clues about what it means to be a laborer (worker) in the harvest. The first thing I saw on my porch that day was the meaning of the Greek word for laborer (worker), *ergates*. It means literally "field hand" or "husbandman"—an agricultural term!

From my farm background, I understood the word *ergates*. As a young kid I sat at the lunch table with men who had come in from the hay fields, their shirts wet with perspiration. When I reached the magical age of thirteen, I graduated from unhitching the wagons to actually lifting bales of alfalfa off the wagons. Sometimes I was assigned to the humid, stifling hay loft, where I carried the heavy bales to the back of the barn, stacking them neatly in a huge pile of 700 or so. It was fun for the first three bales . . . only 697 to go! How I envied the workers on the flatbeds out in the fields where the breeze cooled them. At the end of the day we "men" agreed that it wasn't our backs or arms that hurt as much as our hands, from grabbing the twine of the bales one by one and lifting them into place. Even thick leather gloves didn't numb the pain entirely.

Similarly, Jesus told his disciples that *field workers* are needed. Nothing glamorous about it. You'll work up a sweat, and you'll get tired, and your muscles will ache. *Ergates!* Laboring with Christ is *work!*

Second, I noticed the word *into* in verse 38. The workers are sent *into* the harvest. They are not standing outside the harvest critiquing it or analyzing the best place to work—they are involved with the sheep on the sheep's terms. Just as my dad would not have gotten his hay baled by having the neighbors come over to discuss the crop, so Jesus is not interested in mere talk about the harvest. Workers are involved up to their necks with people. No time to complain about the other workers or the equipment.

Jesus Himself was "in" the harvest. Verse 35 says He was "going through all the cities and villages." He was involved with people. Verse 36 says He "saw" the multitudes. How many times have Christians today been too preoccupied to even "see" the downcast people of our own culture? A laborer is involved with the harvest!

Third, a laborer has compassion for people. Why? Because Jesus had compassion for people. Verse 36 states, "seeing the multitudes, He felt compassion for them." I confess that I do not always have compassion for the multitudes. Instead of viewing people as sheep without a shepherd, I frequently see them as irritating, self-centered, godless TV-watchers who clog crowded highways, talking mindlessly on their cell phones when I am late for church. Blast them! Or, I see the multitudes as hordes of Sunday shoppers filling the Wal-Mart parking lots. Perhaps the multitudes Jesus has compassion for are the people who answer my question: "Who buys this stuff?" as I peruse the gossip magazines at the checkout aisle. I see the multitudes as an irritation—Jesus sees them as sheep needing a shepherd.

According to the book *A Shepherd Looks at Psalm 23*, sheep can become "cast" and must have a shepherd's help.[1] Because of especially thick wool, or being pregnant or overweight, a sheep can become trapped while lying in a shallow depression in the ground. They may struggle for hours to get to their feet, but the struggling only moves them more deeply into the depression, and soon they are on their backs with their feet in the air, helpless. If it is cold or damp, they may die in a few hours. If the weather is warm, it may take a few days. Once a sheep is "cast" it cannot help itself, no matter how hard it tries. That is why there is such urgency in Jesus' story about the shepherd with a hundred sheep (Matthew 18:12-14). Ninety-nine of them were safely in the fold, but one was missing.

The shepherd hurries to find the cast sheep, for he knows time is short. When the shepherd finds the sheep and sets it on its feet, he holds it between his legs, massaging the sheep's legs to get blood circulating again. If he lets it run back to the flock immediately, it will likely fall again. This is a picture of the compassion laborers are to have for the multitude—more concern for the welfare of the sheep than for personal comfort. And certainly, a good shepherd will not consider the sheep an "irritant."

A fourth trait of a biblical laborer centers on the words "send out" in Matthew 9:38. The Greek is even stronger, implying "thrust out" or "impel." A laborer has a sense of being *sent* by God into the harvest. Today the work of personal discipling doesn't command the limelight. You might even be misunderstood by your pastor, who wants you to work on higher-profile programs like teaching Sunday school or serving as a deacon. Because there is so little affirmation, laborers must know God has "sent" them to the harvest.

When I worked at a newspaper, I found myself buried under the pressure of daily copy deadlines and constant phone ringing. "Sell, sell, sell" was the mantra from the boss. But I tried to see beyond that to the fact that God had sent me to the *Daily Tribune* not just to make the newspaper successful, but also to be His laborer. And I had many opportunities to talk with coworkers and clients about Christ. When I left the peace of my home at 7:30 each morning, I knew I was "sent." And that motivated me to keep on despite the pressure. I was a missionary in a harvest. But it was lonely work.

Fifth, laborers are skilled at their tasks. Implied in the word *ergates* is the idea that field hands know *how* to work in the field. In the spiritual field, how many potential workers are frustrated to the point of quitting because they don't have "know-how"? You can have a great vision for ministry and wonderful compassion for the sheep, but if you don't know "how" to share the gospel or "how" to conduct a one-to-one discipling session, you will soon lose heart for laboring.

So what are the skills a spiritual laborer needs? Let me suggest five:

1. Understanding the evangelism process: Can your mentoree make genuine friends and win a hearing for Christ? Over time, can she attract nonbelievers to read the Bible with her?
2. Sharing the gospel effectively: Can your mentoree

share the gospel clearly at the appropriate time? Be careful here; too many believers share Jesus plus the values of their political party. And some over-simplify it by saying, "Just ask Jesus to come in." (For more on evangelism skills, see "Share the Gospel, Not the Baggage" on page 45.)

3. Discipling: Can your mentoree do initial follow up, building the spiritual disciplines into the life of another?

4. Self-motivated daily spiritual feeding: Mentorees at this stage know how to have a daily quiet time, study the Bible, pray, and memorize and meditate on the Scriptures. But have they gotten beyond just doing it legalistically? That is, do they practice these spiritual disciplines out of a deep conviction, need, and desire?

5. Relating to others: Can mentorees relate to people biblically? To nonbelievers? To family? To fellow believers? To their pastors? Are they teamed up with other disciples to reach and disciple still others?

Of course, many more skills could be added. Do some occur to you? Try not to complicate the process or make it overwhelming. These five skills will give you a starting point.

In summary, here is a simple description of a laborer:

- A *worker* in the harvest, but not necessarily in an official position of service.
- *In* the harvest—not sitting on the sidelines. Laborers are up to their necks in people.
- *Compassionate* about the harvest—not irritated by the multitudes.
- *Sent* by Jesus, not merely "putting in a good word" for God every now and then. This implies also that the laborer is secure in Christ and is not in the

harvest for the wrong reasons (for example, to impress the pastor or to make a reputation).

- *Skilled* in the harvest—knowing how to set sheep on their feet again.

A word must be said about discipling and equipping people today who come from dysfunctional backgrounds. And in America that could be half.

Wounded people who are crushed or broken in spirit will not respond well to repeated exhortations to "have a daily quiet time!" Or, "just pray about it!" Or, "share your faith!" Though they might intend to do these disciplines, perhaps mainly to please you, they rarely succeed because they bring their dysfunctional wounds into the Christian life with them. Like a glass ceiling these wounds stop them in character development.

The following illustration helped me understand this for I had been frustrated by the "inability" of one of my dysfunctional (alcoholic father) mentorees to grow in the disciplines.

Imagine a pipe cleaner in a Coca Cola bottle. But the pipe cleaner has been beat up by a dysfunctional family of pipe cleaners and it leans forlornly against the side of the Coke bottle twisted and bent into grotesque shapes—it's been wounded. Plus, it is trapped inside the Coke bottle with little hope of escaping from the small opening at the top.

Imagine the pipe cleaner hearing the gospel and becoming miraculously saved. The glass bottle is shattered into pieces as if by a strong blow from a hammer. The pipe cleaner is free at last! It has escaped from the life to which it was doomed. But as you examine the "new" pipe cleaner closely you see that it is still bent and twisted—oh, not as much, but the wounds are still there.

That simple story helps me realize the task I have in discipling broken people. We must remember that discipling is not simply imparting information and teaching a few skills we call disciplines. The emotions also have to be discipled. Your mentorees may need more love and understanding than you needed because you may not be as wounded as they.

It is crucial that you help them identify their woundedness and coach them in dealing with it. Be understanding and gentle but do not become an enabler. That is not discipleship.

I use the "Bitterness, Regret, and Disappointment" study in the appendix (page 145) to help my mentorees identify their woundings. It's a good start on a long journey. And be sure to share your own woundedness—that will encourage them too—and will help you develop an environment of grace (chapter 13).

In the next chapter, part two, is a good example of helping a wounded brother.

Study Matthew 9:35-38 for yourself to see whether your heart does not begin to beat more and more with the challenge of raising up laborers. And why not start praying every day for laborers? Remember, after Jesus looked on the helpless sheep with compassion, He turned his back on them to address His disciples: "Ask the Lord of the harvest, therefore, to send out workers into his harvest field" (NIV). Without prayer, how much effect can you and I have in raising up laborers for the harvest? This is spiritual work, and God must do it. I have determined to pray daily for laborers—that is His command. Let's start there!

CHAPTER SEVEN

What Makes a Good One-to-One Meeting?

WHEN I AM DRIVING AWAY FROM MEETING WITH MY PROTÉGÉ, I review how our get-together went. First, I consider whether the Holy Spirit was there with us. Nothing can substitute for the presence of God in your ministry. If He is not there, the following seven guidelines are worthless. But if you seek His help ahead of time, asking Him to supervise your meeting, the checklist in this chapter should be helpful. (By the way, don't try to accomplish each item on the list every time you meet.)

1. Did I Listen?

If you talk more than half the time, something is wrong. You have a lot to say, of course, but over time you'll serve your mentoree better by listening than by talking.

Some spiritual leaders interpret this to mean that they shouldn't talk about themselves so much. The old joke "I've talked about me long enough; now it's your turn to talk about me" is only part of it. Don't just refrain from talking about yourself—don't talk at all! Seriously!

You may have learned not to talk about yourself, but can you self-monitor the sermonettes straining to erupt out of your mouth and give your protégé the floor? Stop. Listen. Ask questions. It is more important to be *interested* than interesting! My most convicting verse on self-monitoring my mouth is Proverbs 10:19:

When there are many words, transgression is
    unavoidable,
But he who restrains his lips is wise.

Once I was meeting with a new believer on our regularly scheduled get-together, and fell into the mode of preaching at him. I never noticed how distracted he was. A few minutes before he had to leave, he broke in while I took a breath to say that his nonbelieving father needed surgery. Hesitantly, he ventured the idea of going home to be with his dad after surgery instead of attending a Christian conference with me the following weekend. This was a step of faith for him, because he usually avoided his parents, who were often hostile.

I missed it! Had I asked questions or allowed some silent pauses, I would have honored this tender new believer and let him talk about the difficulty of relating to his parents. And we could have prayed together about his hostile folks. But I was too busy preaching. The proverb I needed was 20:5:

A plan in the heart of man is like deep water,
But a man of understanding draws it out.

Your mentorees have thoughts and feelings buried deep in their hearts that may never surface. You can draw from that deep water simply by asking questions. Also, let there be periods of silence. It's OK for the two of you to be together with silence between you.

2. Did I Touch a Felt Need?

Too often a mentor delivers content that is not relevant to the protégé's current issue. Don't talk about the Christian's blessings in the heavenlies from Ephesians when your mentoree is preparing to leave her husband.

Don't talk about sharing the faith when your mentoree is struggling with hatred for his boss.

My most memorable felt-need session was with Jim. He arrived at the appointed time for our meeting, Bible in hand. We had been having some great times in the Word and had also done some evangelism together. We both looked forward to our biweekly get-togethers.

As Jim arrived, I said, "Change of plans. Get in my car. We're going for a little drive."

"Wow!" Jim said. "An adventure! Where are we going?"

"Can't say," I replied as we pulled out of the driveway, "but I think you're going to like it."

He guessed several destinations as we drove along the icy streets, and finally we pulled up at the shopping mall. "Shall I take my Bible?" he asked.

"No, leave it in the car." Now he was really curious.

We strode into the mall in silence and stopped in front of the best men's clothing store in town. "Here we are!" I announced. Jim looked up at the store and said, "What are we doing here?"

"Jim," I said, "I'm going to buy you a decent pair of dress slacks." Jim immediately glanced down at the pants he was wearing. "No, no," I said. "Those pants are fine, but now that you are finishing at the community college you need to have business dress clothes in addition to your classroom khakis."

Jim was incredulous. "You don't have to do that," he said.

"I know I don't, but I want to, Jim. It's not that you can't afford to buy dress slacks; but I want to do that for you today."

Jim smiled, "Let's go!"

So we picked out Jim's first pair of real men's dress slacks—the kind with zigzag unhemmed edges that need to be tailored. And not only did we fit him in slacks, but also a dress shirt and a matching top-quality sweater. Jim couldn't stop smiling.

What was I trying to do? On the way home in the car I talked with Jim about the fact that despite his alcoholic father and the dysfunctional nonaffirming home he grew up in, he was a man of great value, loved by God. And by me! I wanted to demonstrate to Jim that he was worth making a fuss over. I bought Jim the pants because I loved him. James 2:15-16 applies: "If a brother or sister is without clothing and in need of daily food, and one of you says to them, 'Go in peace, be warmed and be filled,' and yet you do not give them what is necessary for their body, what use is that?" I saw Jim a few weeks later at a party; he was wearing the new outfit. And he was beaming when he caught my eye. Not a word needed to be said.

Jim and I met perhaps twenty times over the course of a couple of years for mentoring. We discussed lots of topics with the Bible between us, and we did a lot of ministry activities, but the mentor–mentoree session we both remember most was the day we went to the mall. Jim needed pants, but his real need was to know the affirming love of God.

Jim recently told me in a letter his memory of the day, "You went to some time, trouble, and expense to help me be successful. And I am grateful. That is also a fitting description of our mentoring relationship over the years."

Your mentorees may not need dress pants, but they have inner felt needs. What can you do to meet them? That is what Jesus would do.

3. Did We Open the Bible?

A few years ago, I had a difficult meeting with a short-term missionary who had been sent back to the U.S. early because of a sexual indiscretion. Wanting to be sensitive, I asked to meet him at an out-of-the-way White Castle, a fast-food joint where the delicious hamburgers are called *sliders*. "Jason" (not his real name) seemed comfortable with the informal surroundings, and before we could order seconds on sliders we were heavily into the struggles he had overseas.

I listened. I asked questions. I probed. I inquired about his parents. I played amateur psychologist. But I was getting nowhere. He was getting frustrated, and I was getting desperate. Near the end of our three-hour meeting, I happened to share a Scripture reference. Finally, with our discussion winding down, I said, "Jason, I feel like I haven't encouraged you at all. Was there anything I said today that was the least bit encouraging?"

He thought a minute. "Yes," he said, "that one Scripture you shared . . . what was that again? That was helpful."

I learned a powerful lesson that day at White Castle: Use the Word, not psychology. It is the Word of God that is quick and powerful—not our words! Not our psychological insights. Not our probing questions.

Of course, you don't want to sprinkle twenty-five Scriptures on your mentoree the way you sprinkle salt on steaming boiled potatoes. But don't leave your meeting without sharing appropriate Scriptures for the issues you've discussed.

Still another time I had a difficult issue to discuss with a mentoree. It was not about his behavior, but his motivations. How would I get into the deep values he held without offending him? I prayed and felt the Lord's leading to bring the matters up to him during the final morning of my visit. But first I felt we should have a time of studying the Bible together and praying.

The Scriptures we looked at were not on the topic I wanted to speak to him about, but as we looked up one verse after another, he freely shared his deep feeling on the very issues I hoped to address. I was able to freely share my own observations, and he accepted them humbly because (I believe) the Bible had prepared his heart. Hebrews 4:12 makes a powerful point: "For the word of God is living and active and sharper than any two-edged sword, and piercing as far as the division of soul and spirit, of both joints and marrow, and able to judge the thoughts and intentions of the heart."

Want to go beyond behavior modification in your ministry? Get into the Bible with your mentorees. Lives will change.

4. Did We Pray Together?

Be sure to leave time for prayer so you don't have to rush through it at the end of your meeting. Let anything else go, but include praying together.

Lorne Sanny, former president of The Navigators, has many stories to tell about Dawson Trotman, founder of The Navigators and Sanny's mentor. Trotman was known for his captivating personality and zeal for God. He deeply influenced dozens of Christian ministry leaders like Bill Bright, Billy Graham, and Jim Rayburn in the 1940s and 50s. Sanny spent thousands of hours with Trotman, who discipled him, trained him in leadership, and equipped him to lead The Navigators as his successor.

I once heard Sanny say what he remembered most about Dawson: "Our prayer times together. Sometimes when we lifted our heads from prayer you could almost touch the presence of God. It was that real."

Praying together is difficult if you meet in a public area, like a restaurant or your protégé's cubicle. While it may be acceptable to bow your heads before a meal, you may not want to use a public area for an extended time of prayer, particularly if it involves confessing sins! You also must consider the comfort level of your mentoree. Here are a few guidelines I use:

- Go to his car to pray for a few minutes.
- Walk around the parking lot or up the street and pray while you walk.
- Offer a "ten-second prayer" as you walk him to his car or just before leaving his office. ("Ten seconds" means ten seconds!)

Isn't one of your goals in mentoring to bring another closer to Christ? What better way to do it than to pray together? We must never become too sophisticated to pray with one another. Remember Jesus' words in Matthew 18:20: "For where two or three have gathered together in My name, I am there in their midst."

5. Did We Laugh?

Laughing together is a signal to both of you that the time you spend together is genuine—not an artificial spiritual exercise. As I look back on those who have met with me over the years, I can assure you that we did plenty of laughing, a lot of it at my expense! Having fun together is a good relationship builder. But even more practically, people long to laugh—really laugh! Also, some of the material you will cover with your mentoree will be pretty serious. Laughter is needed to balance that.

You've probably read that a child of five laughs many more times a day than an adult. Remember the proverb "A merry heart doeth good like a medicine" (Proverbs 17:22, KJV). Bring laughter into your one-to-one meetings—not by telling jokes, but by sharing your lives. God will see to it that your hearts are merry!

6. Was I Vulnerable?

There is great power in revealing our foibles. I like King David in the Old Testament because we see him without the artist's retouching brush—goof-ups and all. That encourages me!

Do your mentorees see you as you really are, or do you put on a happy face and determine not to show weakness? If so, you are modeling a false view of the Christian life and you may be promoting legalism. Your mentorees have problems with lovelessness, dishonesty, lust, greed, discipline, arrogance, and more. And unless you tell them you struggle with those things, too, they will assume that "successful Christians" have conquered all the stuff they deal with daily. They'll wonder if they will ever "get it." Why are others so victorious and they are not? Let them see your strengths, for sure, but let them see the other you, too—the one that struggles with hard character issues.

Though He had no sinfulness to reveal, Jesus was vulnerable with His disciples. In the Garden of Gethsemane, He poured out His heart to God with deep anguish—with "loud crying and tears," according to Hebrews 5:7. He didn't try to cover up His feelings from the Twelve.

Similarly, Paul says to his protégé Timothy, "But thou hast *fully known* my doctrine, manner of life, purpose, faith, longsuffering, charity, patience, persecutions, afflictions, which came to me at Antioch, at Iconium, at Lystra" (2 Timothy 3:10-11, KJV). Note the words *fully known*. Timothy was not shielded from the difficulties Paul faced. Not only did he get doctrine from Paul, he got a firsthand look at Paul's purpose—his motivations! He saw Paul sticking with it even in hard times—his longsuffering. Paul held nothing back from young Timothy.

You don't need to advertise your weaknesses; they will come out in due time. Just don't try to cover them up. Being human with feet of clay is not unforgivable, but putting on an image that you don't struggle will mislead your mentorees about Christian maturity. That was what the Pharisees tried to do. Be vulnerable.

7. Did We Serve Christ Together?

Your mentorees will grow rapidly if you can engage in ministry with them now and then rather than sitting in Taco John's every time. Why not take her with you as you share the gospel with a friend or visit people through your church's evangelism calling program? Or what about taking your protégé to the hospital with you to visit a sick person? Or you could help a widow with her storm windows. You might even take a missions trip together.

Jesus did this constantly. In fact, He taught His mentorees truth in the midst of constant ministry. The disciples learned great lessons about the kingdom by the "with Him" principle. Not only did they observe Jesus in action, but they were asked to participate, too. Jesus sent them out two by two before you and I would have thought they were ready. When the multitude needed food, he said to Peter, "You feed them!" Peter's answer—"What are these for so many?"—revealed his limited view of Jesus. This on-the-job training in close association with Jesus prepared the disciples to take on the task of the Great Commission in just three years.

Similarly, look for opportunities to dive into ministry together. One of the best ways to teach discipleship is to take a mentoree on a ministry trip to another location. As you enter a church class or someone else's Bible study, you are now "the experts." Your mentorees will realize they must now respond to God's call as they present their testimonies or share the Scriptures. You'll see their fears and insecurities, and they will see yours. Let them rise to the challenge—they will grow in their ability to trust God.

By doing ministry together I discover what my protégés know, what they feel strongly about, and what gifts and skills God has given them. I also find out what they *don't* know and where their convictions and skills are weak. Plus, because ministry together to others is not "rehearsal," our friendship leaps ahead. To use a military term, it's "live bullets," not merely training.

By doing ministry together you'll not only enhance your mentoring, you'll also be following in the steps of Jesus as you apply the "with him" or "with her" principle!

Related to these seven benchmarks for an effective one-to-one meeting are five pitfalls—errors in thinking about one-to-one ministry in general. These pitfalls are not so much mistakes in *how* we do one-to-one work but our *attitudes* toward it. Have you ever been on the receiving end of some of these misguided views of discipling?

Problem-Solving
In the past, I'd sometimes quiz protégés on various topics, searching for their felt needs. I'd zero in on problems like mosquitoes zero in on Lutherans at a Minnesota picnic. I'd ask about relationships with parents, use of time,

secret thought life. As soon as they revealed a struggle I'd rush in with wise counsel and a verse of Scripture. They would thank me, and we'd dismiss until next time.

Can you see the downside of this type of "equipping"? Gradually, your mentoree becomes as hesitant as a missionary on a fundraising call. This approach might touch an urgent need occasionally, but it also puts the mentor–mentoree relationship into a counselor–counselee mode. One has the answers; one needs answers. It also twists discipling into a problem-oriented view of the Christian life.

Listening Only

The second error is letting the mentoree talk endlessly (better than you talking endlessly!) until he finally asks you a question. I remember meeting with one mature disciple for months, but he was a talker. He was in the equipping stage and had a solid walk with Christ. Because he was frustrated in business and considering going into overseas missions, I encouraged his talk, thinking he needed a listening ear. But he obsessed on the topic of God's will for his life hour after hour. He covered the same ground each time we met.

I had a couple of Bible study ideas we could have pursued, but I was waiting for him to talk himself out. He never did! If I had suggested we open our Bibles to see what it said about work and missions, he would have stopped talking and dived into the Word with me. But I never did. I missed an opportunity.

Repeating the How-Tos

It's wonderful if your mentorees know the how-tos of quiet time, Bible study, prayer, and sharing their faith, but they need more from you than merely learning how to perfect these methods. In the equipping stage they can always improve their quiet times or study methods, but constantly reviewing the disciplines communicates legalism. Do some mentors keep revisiting the Bible intake methods because they don't know what else to do?

Your mentorees will develop a greater appreciation for the basics as you open their minds to new topics that touch a felt need — topics like overcoming resentment and bitterness, why we repeat sins, and growing in marriage. And if they came from a dysfunctional background you will lose their interest if you cover only the how-tos. Their emotional pain will cause them not even to hear you!

Graduating Prematurely

After a few months you may be tempted to tell your mentoree, "It's time for you to bloom and multiply," but she may not thrive spiritually after leaving the environment of Bible study and one-to-one sessions you have created for her. She may not be able to reproduce that same environment — particularly those mentorees who come from harsh, dysfunctional homes or torrid backgrounds. Be skeptical of "twelve-week" disciples who can now run the church! How are they doing on the habits of a lifelong laborer discussed in Chapter 6? Be careful not to graduate the mentoree until it is time.

Fruit-Inspecting

Without a plan to take your mentorees to the next step, you might revert to "inspecting" to see if your mentorees are faithful in quiet times, church attendance, and winning souls. Mentorees catch on to your motive immediately if you are checking up on their "performance."

Let's review what makes a good one-to-one meeting:

- Did I listen?
- Did I touch a felt need?
- Did we open the Bible?
- Did we pray together?
- Did we laugh?
- Was I vulnerable?
- Did we serve Christ together?
- Am I avoiding attitudinal errors like
  problem-solving, listening only, repeating the

how-tos, graduating prematurely, and fruit-inspecting?

Applying these checkpoints and avoiding the pitfalls will not guarantee excellent one-to-one meetings, but you'll more effectively meet the needs of your mentoree. Should you prepare for a meeting? Yes, but don't fixate on the topic you prepared. Your mentoree may have a father who needs surgery. Be flexible!

CHAPTER EIGHT

Leadership Blind Spots in Discipling: Jesus' Nine-Point Checklist

THE INTEGRITY OF NATIONALLY KNOWN CHRISTIAN LEADERS is examined by everyone—the news media, the elder board, the finance committee. But who checks the integrity of millions of lay leaders who guide weekly Bible studies, teach Sunday school, and disciple new believers?

Integrity problems in *my* ministry? I've never "borrowed" pencils from church, flirted with the organist, or photocopied copyrighted material (at least it didn't say it was copyrighted). Integrity problems? Not me.

But then I began to notice Matthew 23, where Jesus excoriates the Pharisees. In the past I figured Jesus' stinging accusations didn't apply to me. I saw nothing more than a routine warning against professional hypocrisy—something my pastor should read. To my chagrin, I found nine stinging accusations that *did* apply to me!

You may not find the ABC sound truck parked in your driveway tomorrow morning, but your integrity is crucial to your discipling ministry. Rather than be scrutinized by Barbara Walters, I invite you to rate yourself against Jesus' nine guideposts for ministry integrity from Matthew 23.

1. Does Your Behavior Match Your Teaching?

"The scribes and the Pharisees have seated themselves in the chair of Moses; therefore all that they
tell you, do and observe, but do not do according to
their deeds; for they say things and do not do
them." (Matthew 23:2-3)

In Jesus' day, synagogues had a stone seat at the front
where the teacher sat to teach. Unlike today, you didn't
stand up to teach; you sat down. Though they were recognized as teachers, the Pharisees' actions did not match
their words. Even so, Jesus said, "Do all they tell you. But
don't copy their behavior." Are disciplers subject to the
same requirements? For example, I challenge others to
share their faith—but do I? Albert Schweitzer, the leg-
endary missionary doctor of Africa, said, "Example is not
the main thing in influencing others—it is the only
thing."

2. Do You Tie Up Heavy Burdens for Your Pupils?

"They tie up heavy loads and lay them on men's
shoulders, but they themselves are unwilling to move
them with so much as a finger." (23:4)

I was the speaker at a weekend conference in the north
woods of Wisconsin when a discouraged college student
approached me. In a few minutes, I would ascend the
platform to stand (not sit) behind an imposing pulpit to
give my third and final talk—a stiff challenge to obey
God. It promised to be a barn-burner.

Clutching her Bible and notes, the student's counte-
nance was full of frustration. She asked, "Why is it that
every talk is a challenge? I need encouragement."

I had two talks prepared that morning—a message on
hope, only partially prepared (and a little "fluffy," I

thought), and a challenging talk on discipleship. I didn't think the hope talk was powerful enough, so I left it in my room.

That overwhelmed student was the Lord's messenger. I hastily retrieved the partially prepared hope message. Though the delivery was not great, I don't have to tell you which message the Lord used most that weekend.

We can overchallenge our conscientious mentorees in small groups or in one-to-one discipling. We usually feel more useful if we give a challenging sermonette (usually to pray more or to share Christ more). One of the guys I'm discipling calls that "pounding"! It's easier to pound than to genuinely encourage. Your mentorees who come from a crushing dysfunctional background can't handle pounding!

But Jesus goes further. What does the leader do to help the pupils carry the load? The Pharisees would not lift a finger. These days, if I give a heavy challenge, I offer resources. For example, when challenging people to have a daily quiet time, I give them *Seven Minutes with God* from NavPress or my paragraph-a-day outline of Mark's gospel.

3. Do You Try to Impress People?

> "But they do all their deeds to be noticed by men;
> for they broaden their phylacteries and lengthen the
> tassels of their garments." (23:5)

The Jews were instructed in Numbers 15:38-39 to make tassels for the corners of their clothing—not for decoration, but as a reminder to "remember all the commandments." Phylacteries were small leather boxes worn on the arm or forehead containing four Old Testament texts. To show their holiness, the Pharisees lengthened their tassels and enlarged the leather boxes. The more showy, the more holy.

Even though I've never worn phylacteries, the lure of being "noticed by men" has been a struggle. Once I was privileged to share a meal at a busy weekend conference with a veteran missionary from Japan. Determined to advertise my great humility, I leaped from my chair to serve hot coffee to the table guests. Others offered to help, but I didn't want anyone else to steal my humble sideshow. As I hurriedly returned from the coffee steamer, my fingers strung awkwardly through three cups, I imagined what the missionary was thinking: "What a humble young man — and so quick, too."

It was then that I accidentally poured steaming coffee down the back of the fiancée of my Bible study leader. She screamed. The veteran missionary and others jumped to their feet and offered napkins. Chaos reigned for twenty seconds at table 12. The entire dining room was hushed. I made an impression all right. People-pleasing acts of service are not for the one being served, but to bolster the ego of the insecure doer of good deeds.

Another technique for impressing others is to "spiritu-alize" conversations with comments like, "The Lord told me to do this" or "This morning, during my ninety minutes of prayer. . . ." In Matthew 6, Jesus said that those who live to impress others will "have their reward" — the fleeting thought that crosses your mind, "People think I'm cool." That's the reward! Enjoy it! It's over!

How can you tell if you are a people-pleaser? How do you feel when you are not recognized? If you are resentful, chances are you were trying to impress somebody. Identify that somebody, and you're on your way to recovery.

4. Do You Delight When Your Pupils Surpass You?

"You shut off the kingdom of heaven from people; for you do not enter in yourselves, nor do you allow those who are entering to go in." (23:13)

Because of their legalistic outlook, the Pharisees held back kingdom-seekers. They could not take people farther than they themselves had gone. How about us? Don't hold back your pupils' spiritual growth just because you have not experienced what they are experiencing.

During the Korean War, a young Marine named Charles was discipled by a group of Navigator fellow Marines. He was taught the basics of studying the Bible, memorizing Scripture, and sharing his faith. He showed great promise and was encouraged to blossom. What a shame it would have been if these Navigator servicemen had tried to limit Chuck Swindoll!

If those we lead grow only to our level, we are in big trouble. Let's launch our people way beyond us! I think 2 Corinthians 1:24 says it well: "Not that we lord it over your faith, but are workers with you for your joy." Don't dominate them — help them experience joy!

5. Are You Molding People in Your Image, or Christ's?

"You travel around on sea and land to make one proselyte; and when he becomes one, you make him twice as much a son of hell as yourselves." (23:15)

The Pharisees molded their converts in their own images. Like spiritual father, like spiritual son — it was a control issue. They did not allow their followers to think differently than they did.

In my early days of ministry, I was flattered when my little "gang" of followers quoted me. But as they grew, I found myself feeling insecure when they listened to other teachers and even displayed their own opinions. Later, I was corrected by the large-heartedness and Christ-centeredness of the apostle Paul, who told the Corinthians: "By the grace God has given me, I laid a foundation as an expert builder, and someone else is building on it. But each one should be careful how he builds. For no one can lay any foundation other than the one already laid, which is Jesus Christ" (1 Corinthians 3:10-11, NIV).

To avoid building people in your image, always point them to Jesus Christ. Though we are called to "make disciples," they are to be disciples of Christ—not disciples of you! In the end, He's the only trustworthy model for us all!

6. Am I in It for the Power?

"You devour widows' houses, and [for] a pretense you make long prayers." (Matthew 23:14)

It is easy to accuse TV preachers of being in ministry for the money, but what about us? A friend recently told me of a Christian leader who invited him over for "fellowship," but the real purpose was to recruit him into a multilevel marketing plan.

Do you see ministry as an opportunity for networking? Do you bring your business cards to church? What about nonmonetary rewards? As a lay discipler, you are not on a ministry payroll, but public recognition often accompanies success. Do you use your discipling group to boost your ego? Do not work for the power or prestige that goes along with being a "gifted leader." Would you serve if no one recognized your ministry?

7. Are You Majoring on the Majors?

"For you tithe mint and dill and cummin, and have neglected the weightier provisions of the law: justice and mercy and faithfulness." (23:23)

Can you imagine sitting at your kitchen table culling out 10 percent of your potatoes or sunflower seeds? The Pharisees did. Seeds can be measured. But they missed the bigger, hard-to-measure issues like justice.

What about us? Are we meticulous in minor measurable things, but neglectful of important issues that are not so measurable? Here are some possibilities:

- You can develop masterful multicolor Bible studies—but your kids fear your anger at home.
- You can give a wonderful three-point testimony—but you secretly browse soft porn on cable.
- You never miss a quiet time, but you exaggerate tax deductions.

I once confronted a leader in our college ministry about her poor relationship with her parents, who admittedly were difficult to get along with. After much prayer, she finally agreed to take a Christmas trip with them to improve their relationship. I was proud of her.

"How did it go?" I asked optimistically when she returned.

"Oh, fine, I guess," she sighed. "I sat in the front seat organizing my memory verses. They didn't talk to me much."

There is an appropriate time to focus on organizing your memory verses or sort out cummin! But she was guilty of majoring on a minor at the expense of showing Christ's love to her parents. Mercy was robbed during that trip.

8. Are You Keeping Up Appearances to Cover Indulgence?

> "For you clean the outside of the cup and of the dish, but inside they are full of robbery and self-indulgence." (23:25)

I don't like this word *indulgence*. The Greek word is *akrasia*, and it means "want of self-restraint" (*Strong's Concordance*).

In Russia in the 1980s, members of the Communist Party didn't stand in long lines to buy bread. The leaders indulged themselves while the followers suffered. If you and I cannot restrain ourselves in private habits, those who look to us for leadership will look elsewhere. Good leaders are followed in public because they can lead themselves in private.

Ask yourself: Have I displayed any areas of secret indulgence today? Did I

- give in to my love affair with jelly donuts?
- indulge in titillating TV (just to see what's on)?
- browse through nasty websites on the Internet?
- drift to the mall for shopping therapy?

Those areas in which I allow myself indulgences are the areas in which I am silent in ministry. I wouldn't want to be a hypocrite!

9. Do You Consider Yourself Superior to Others?

> "'If we had been living in the days of our fathers, we would not have been partners with them in shedding the blood of the prophets.'" (23:30)

The Pharisees had a bad case of spiritual pride, and you and I are not immune to it. When we see poor leadership, we sniff, "I would never do that." That's spiritual pride. We are capable of any mistake the worst of sinners has ever made! To say we are not is to misunderstand our depravity and telegraph our superior attitude.

Two hundred years ago a detachment of Revolutionary War soldiers was felling trees to construct a bridge. Their officer was urging them on, but progress was slow. An unknown rider approached, studied the predicament, and asked the officer why he was not laboring with the men. "Me, Sir? Why, I am a corporal!" he countered. Immediately, the stranger dismounted and joined in the work until it was finished. Then he rode off as unobtrusively as he had come. The unknown rider? General George Washington.[1]

Who checks the integrity of lay disciplers? You may

have a mentor or a support group, but many don't. Even with an accountability group, it is easy to dodge being pinned down. (And you are probably leading the group anyway!)

Ultimately, our integrity in personal ministry comes from daily honesty with Christ. Don't depend on someone else to keep you ethical. Start now by praying through Jesus' checklist to the Pharisees — you'll attract the respect of followers!

CHAPTER NINE

Leading Small Groups: Five Mistakes to Avoid

In discipling, you must do more than meet one-to-one with your mentorees. They need the influence of others who are growing in Christ. A small study group provides a platform where they can learn from one another even at different stages of spiritual maturity. They will likely learn as much from one another as from you. Just as off-speed pitches enhance a pitcher's fastball, so your small group enhances your one-to-one ministry.

However, leading a Bible study group has perils. My guess is that you've been in small groups and have sometimes come home vowing never to go again! Here are five mistakes I've made in leading small groups—we should avoid these like a wet Golden Retriever.

1. Talking Too Much

Some groups I've led were nothing more than a mini-worship service with me presenting insightful sermonettes. After all, I learned a lot during my preparation, and others needed to hear it! As the study members leave, they tell me what a blessing the study is. I beam. What great folks!

But at bedtime, in a more sober mood, I ponder: "What if a timekeeper kept track of the minutes each member spoke during a two-hour evening Bible study?" Mine too often go something like this:

- Greetings, snacks, small talk: 20 minutes
- Bill, assistant leader: 6 minutes
- Sally didn't say much tonight: 3 minutes
- Bob seemed awfully silent: 4 minutes
- Joe had an excellent question, but it was off the subject; wonder if it got answered: 10 minutes
- Jane didn't talk at all, seemed disconnected
- Susan rambled about her kids: 5 minutes
- Closing prayer and saying goodbye: 15 minutes
- My comments and sermonettes: 57 minutes

The Bible study leader talking 57 minutes of a 120-minute gathering of six friends is way too much! More important than the leader sharing riveting sermonettes is the opportunity for the members to share their thoughts, feelings, and convictions (or lack thereof). A good leader will persistently draw out the views of the members, encouraging them to deal with the text and its implications for daily living. It is more important that a study member share frustrations with the text than to hear a wonderful exegesis from the leader.

How about you? Are you talking too much?

2. Asking Artificial Questions
In my early days of leading Bible studies, I read somewhere that a good study leader asks penetrating questions to incite the members to a rousing discussion. So I laboriously prepared a string of outstanding questions for my next study with new believers.

The first question bombed. No one responded. So I gave the answer. Then I asked my second question. Nothing. Finally someone said, "Scott, why don't you just tell us what we need to know." My heart sank.

My error was in preparing artificial questions that did not address the members' needs. I also assumed that the members had deeply studied the text like I had. But they hadn't.

Be real. Let your members be real. Genuineness is key.

3. No Preparation, or Too Much Preparation

I confess that some of the best Bible studies I've led were ones for which I did no preparation. I'm not sure why, except that maybe I was more in tune with the Holy Spirit. But I also confess that some of the best studies I've led were ones for which I was thoroughly prepared. Go figure. The key is being sensitive to God.

In your preparation, let the study speak to you personally, rather than view yourself as one who has already mastered the material and is now merely preparing teaching notes. Let God speak to you first.

Second, think through the material from the members' perspectives. Anticipate questions the study will raise with them. For example, if you are studying marriage, consider: Have any study members been divorced? Did some have premarital sex? What kind of marriage did their parents have? Their history will color what they learn from the study and how you guide the discussion. Thinking through the study from their perspective may protect you from embarrassing moments.

4. No Fun or Creativity

How many studies have you attended where the study leader laboriously went through the study questions one by one, asking members to recite their answers? Or have you gone around the study circle with each member reading a verse, then asked, "What does that verse mean to you?" Boring. We can do better than that. Don't allow your members to be bored! Here are two suggestions to help keep things lively:

Flip Chart

If you're studying in a home with people who are comfortable with one another, consider bringing a flip chart. It is cumbersome to cram a flip chart into the back seat of your Toyota, especially on a windy evening, but it is worth it. I'm guessing half the people in the world are visual learners. Use the flip chart to pose a problem the study brought up or draw a diagram to illustrate a key verse. Have a member "go to the board" to explain an important point.

The flip chart takes the focus off you as the leader. It is an objective third party that keeps the study on track. (Caution: A flip chart may be threatening to those who associate it with being in school. It can also put you in the role of teacher, but you can avoid that by not sermonizing and by having others go to the board.)

Object Lesson

Here's a simple example of an object lesson. In a study on faith I posed a question on the flip chart: "How do you know if you have enough faith?" After discussion, the group concluded we would never have enough. Then we looked at Matthew 17:20, where Jesus pointed out that faith the size of a mustard seed can move mountains. Next, I produced from Alma's spice cabinet a bottle of mustard seeds. One by one the members took a tiny seed out of the small-necked bottle and taped it onto an index card. Then they wrote their favorite verse about faith on the card and kept it in their Bible as a bookmark.

Simplistic? Perhaps. But the study members still commented on it weeks later.

Once I brought a small stone and a piece of redwood bark to the study. At the beginning of the study I placed both the stone and the bark into a bowl of water as everyone watched. I didn't explain it, but said we'd check the bowl at the end of the study.

That simple act created *mystique*. The members caught on before the study was over that the wood absorbed the water but the stone did not. The lesson: are we "absorbing" the Word, or are we inundated like the stone but not letting it speak to us?

Try it! Pack a flip chart or bring a simple object to create interest and make a point.

5. Failure to Encourage Application

The Bible was not written primarily to fill our brains, but to change our lives. If you end without discussing how the study will make a difference in daily living, you have done your members a disservice. With adequate time remaining, bring the study to a close by asking: "OK, so what! How will these passages make a difference in our lives Monday morning after you've had a kid vomit on the new carpet and after the boss plops a surprise project on your desk?"

Silence. It's OK to have silence. Let the Spirit of God work. That shows you are serious in asking the question. Encourage the members to be as specific as they can. Don't allow an overgeneralization: "My application is to be a better person." That is a wonderful intent, but follow it up with, "Can you tell us a couple of specific ways God has spoken to you about being a better person?"

Be sure to leave enough time to discuss application thoroughly. Too often I haven't watched the clock closely enough and have asked for applications when the members were worried about getting their babysitters home on time. Don't hurry the application time. Make it the highlight.

And be sure to end with the members praying— unless it is a group of nonbelievers or new believers who are not yet comfortable praying aloud. Praying together further connects members with God and one another. But don't let the prayer time drag on.

How much time should you allow for a study group meeting? At an office or restaurant, you'll do well to have thirty to forty minutes of actual Bible discussion. But in a home, you can easily spend sixty to eighty minutes, not to mention time for snacking, prayer, and fellowship. With nonbelievers, I go no more than an hour, including extras. At any study, follow the adage of my junior high track coach, who saw me practicing running hurdles: "Quit while you still want to run one more!" Similarly, dismiss the study while members still want to discuss more.

CHAPTER TEN

How to Lovingly Confront:
When Christians Behave Badly

DO YOU ENJOY CORRECTING A FELLOW BELIEVER WHO'S behaving badly? I don't, and I don't know anyone who does. Though Scripture exhorts us to love our mentorees enough to confront them, is it worth the risk? And who are we to preach! Couldn't they accuse us of bad behavior, too?

An overarching guideline for confronting is a phrase from Ephesians 4:15: *speaking the truth in love.* Biblical confrontation *is not easy* and *should not be easy.* Both parties experience an ache in their hearts, and I'm not suggesting the ache can be skirted. It is often as painful for the confronter as the confronted. If we find confronting easy and look forward to it, we probably have a bigger problem!

But what about the high cost of *not* confronting? I once heard a veteran leader say about a forty-year-old being considered for a promotion, "He still has that anger problem he exhibited fifteen years ago. Why didn't someone help him then?" That's the high price we pay for "minding our own business!"

When I consider lovingly correcting a protégé, obstacles appear before me like huge, jagged icebergs. Are you held back by these questions?

- What do I say? Shall I hint?
- What if she refuses my counsel and gossips about me?
- Shouldn't the pastor handle this?
- When? Shall I wait until she errs again?

The biggest obstacle may be America's preoccupation with "tolerance." We dare not judge another's religion, sexual orientation, political leanings, or tattoos. We tolerate everything except intolerance.

"Judge not, that ye be not judged," Jesus said (Matthew 7:1, KJV). Eric Clapton in "Before You Accuse Me" sings, "Before you accuse me, take a look at yourself." And guests on late-night talk shows piously preach that we must not impose our values on others. Isn't America a great country? (Cue applause.)

This popular cultural view affects disciplers too. We are reticent to challenge anyone on anything—though gossip is permitted, especially about the pastor's wife! But what do the Scriptures teach? Jesus expanded His "judge not" teaching in Matthew 7 with this response to His critics in John 7:24: "Do not judge according to appearance, but judge with righteous judgment."

To strip life of all analysis will produce a society with no standards. Nothing is "wrong." Everything is of equal value. Paul also throws a wrench into the "judge not" theology in 1 Corinthians 5:12, where he tells the Corinthians to take responsibility for sinning church members: "For what have I to do with judging outsiders? Do you not judge those who are within the church?"

Tolerance indeed. Furthermore, what effect does tolerating wrongdoing among believers have on nonbelievers? They consider it hypocrisy that we criticize them but put up with nonsense within our fellowships.

Tolerance? Yes, but we also have a responsibility to admonish those among us. Is it possible we make admonition too difficult? The Scriptures can help us overcome the following three major misconceptions.

Misconception 1: It's Not My Responsibility

Admonishing is a job for pastors—or for those gifted in counseling. Or is it the responsibility of all believers? In Romans 15:14, Paul says the Romans are "full of goodness, filled with all knowledge and able also to *admonish* one another" (emphasis added). Goodness and knowledge are not enough; the members of the body are expected to admonish one another. Indeed, I believe the ability to admonish is one sign of a fellowship's maturity.

Misconception 2: Confronting Is the Same As Scolding

The Greek word translated "admonish" in Romans 15:14 is *noutheteo,* and it means to put in mind, to caution, to call attention to, to reprove gently, or to warn. It does not mean to scold.

In Titus 2:15, Paul exhorts Titus to "speak and exhort and reprove with all authority. Let no one disregard you." The word translated "reprove" (*elengcho*) means to expose or to bring to light. Similar to *noutheteo,* it does not imply scolding.

I learned a valuable lesson on biblical reproving during Saturday morning chore time when our children were young. Cleaning their room was at the top of the list for our young daughters, Jane and Beth. One Saturday they reported back faithfully (and more quickly than I thought possible) that they had cleaned their room. They wondered whether they could now go out and play with their friends, who were circling the house like turkey vultures waiting for the warden to release the inmates.

"Sure," I said. "Thanks for pitching in with such a quick job." Off they went to join the vultures. But minutes later I walked by their room: it was a mess, though the beds were neatly made and the toys were put away. I summoned the inmates back into the prison for a chat with the warden. Though I dreaded it, I mentally prepared a lecture on obeying your parents.

"So, this room is clean?" questioned the warden sternly.

"Yes, Father. We cleaned it just like you asked," the two inmates chorused tentatively. Silence.

"But look at the clothes lying on the floor, and the dust bunnies under the bed are the size of cocker spaniels," the warden protested.

"Oh, we didn't know that you wanted the clothes picked up and the dust bunnies collected. We thought making the beds and picking up the toys meant the room was clean."

The warden learned an important lesson that day: Reproof involves reinterpreting the instructions—not scolding. Beth and Jane did not have bad hearts; they were not rebellious; they simply did not understand my definition of "Clean your room." The next Saturday their room was cleaned to the warden's satisfaction the first time. Reproof enabled them to understand the standards. No scolding needed.

Misconception 3: You Must Deal with Motives

In past years I tried to identify the offender's motives—not merely their behaviors. I wanted to shrewdly deal with "core issues." For example, if a Bible study member was constantly late for the meeting, I'd guess pride as the core issue. If the kids forgot to feed the dog, I'd assume deep-seated rebellion. If a boss spoke bluntly to me, it was because his dad didn't come to his Little League ballgames!

But my "psychological sleuthing" abused the offenders. How could I know *why* they demonstrated a certain behavior? Galatians 6:1 says we are to restore a brother or sister who is caught in a "trespass." The guilty party might confess the motives if restored in an honoring way, but we are to speak to the trespass (behavior) we observe. Don't play Dr. Freud. Let God deal with motives, and that might not involve you.

Now, how to admonish: Let's say you observe a mentoree repeatedly engaging in destructive criticism. He needs to be confronted lovingly, you know him well, and he respects you. Here are four tips from four Scriptures.

1. Do It in Private

> "If your brother *sins,* go and reprove him in *private; if* he listens to you, you have won your brother." (Matthew 18:15, emphasis added)

Admonition in the presence of others is potentially destructive and should be used only as the last resort with an uncooperative offender (verses 16-17). In addition, your reproof should be addressed to the offender directly—not to others. It is easy even for well-meaning mentors to tell others about the offender's sins (as a prayer request!). Talk *to* people—not *about* people.

Note the second *if* in verse 15. There is no guarantee the offender will listen. It's a risk to admonish, but consider the high cost of *not* admonishing. Will he stop on his own?

And notice the word *sins.* What sin has been committed? Though his spiked hairdo or the funny way he laughs may annoy you, neither qualifies as sin. Let it go!

2. Don't Flatter

> Whoever flatters his neighbor is spreading a net for his feet. (Proverbs 29:5, NIV)

Sometimes, in preparing to confront, we are tempted to "butter up" the unsuspecting offender with flattery to make the admonition less painful. But the offender sees through your "compliments" and feels manipulated.

Christian literature today tells us to be generous with praise and stingy with criticism. Agreed. But using praise to grease the skids is demeaning. Sometimes you can point out to the offender that her strength is a weakness that goes too far. For example, if the strength of being forthright is overdone, it can lead to being demanding.

3. Don't Hint

> I did not shrink from declaring to you anything that
> was profitable. (Acts 20:20)

Too often we hint or joke about the offense, hoping the
offender will get the point and genuinely repent. We've
done our duty—he just didn't catch on. That is "shrinking"
from our responsibility and does not honor the offender.
Usually, we hint because we are afraid to be honest.

I ask myself: *Will my honestly sharing with the offender
bring him some profit if he catches my point?* Though the
offender may feel hurt at first, he will be grateful if he
"profits." I find that writing down specific behavior observations and reading them to the offender keeps me from
shrinking back. And he is honored because he knows
exactly what behavior is in question.

4. Keep a Spirit of Gentleness

> Brethren, even if a man is caught in any trespass, you
> who are spiritual, restore such a one in a spirit of
> gentleness; looking to yourselves, lest you too be
> tempted. (Galatians 6:1)

"You who are spiritual" does not imply "you who are
superior." We are not immune from committing the same
sin we are correcting. And we are to "restore"—not con-
demn—with humility. But be sure to do it! If we wait
until we have it all together in our walk with Christ, we
will never restore anyone.

Let me summarize with four words from 2 Timothy
3:16—*teach, reprove, correct, encourage.* This is what the Bible
does with us, and it provides a strategy for helping others.

Teach. Before you can admonish, ask: *Does the
offender know the teaching?*

Does your protégé understand the Bible's teaching
about a critical spirit? If you suspect she does not, do a

short Bible study with her on the topic. That may solve the problem. Don't reprove until the teaching is clear—remember the dust bunnies!

Reprove. As mentioned earlier, the word here means to expose, to tell a fault, or to convince. Once taught, it is time to *expose* the offender to the fact that her behavior does not match the teaching—just like I did with my daughters on Saturday chores. Perhaps something like this:

"Sheila, will you allow me permission to mention something that might be helpful in your Christian testimony?" If she says OK, add, "I couldn't help but notice that your talk at the last two Bible studies involved criticism of your church. I could be wrong, but I thought I heard you say the pastor's wife is a bore. That seems inconsistent with your Christian testimony. Am I missing something? Do you see what I'm saying?"

You have not scolded Sheila. You have pointed out a specific example in which her behavior does not match her Christian testimony. Then keep silent and allow Sheila to comment. Does she agree with your observation? If she is close to Christ, she might admit the error and even confess the motivation.

If you think her response will be negative, if your relationship bridge is not strong, or if she will not give you permission to speak into her life, you may want to wait. However, if you have formalized the mentoring arrangement she may have already given you permission.

Correct. Don't leave it at reproving. Go on to the more positive area of correcting: "Sheila, I struggle with criticism too. Let's determine in upcoming studies to avoid criticism of the pastor's wife or anyone—and we won't chime in if others do it. OK? And maybe in our next one to one get-together we could review a short passage of Scripture on exchanging criticism with edification."

Also, move forward. Don't dwell on the problem—focus on solving it in bite-size steps. But we're not done yet.

Encourage. This fourth word may be the most important. Most Bibles translate this passage "training in righteousness." But the Greek word used here for training (*pathos*) means "experience, usually painful." *Painful* doesn't fit here, but *experience* does. When I "train" my hair to fall a certain way I repeatedly reinforce or "encourage" it by smoothing it over and over. We can do the same reinforcing with our mentorees.

After Sheila has been *taught* the right behavior, after she has been *reproved* to understand the teaching better, after she has been *corrected* to get on the right path again, then it is time to reinforce the teaching with *encouragement* of the right conduct.

Social scientists tell us that they get better results by reinforcing good behavior than by constantly correcting. Going back to our example, you could encourage Sheila by telling her, "Way to go! Your comments about the pastor were uplifting in Bible study last night. Good work."

When giving reinforcing affirmation, avoid general statements, like telling Sheila she's a great person. Generalities don't encourage and often come across as insincere. Find specific actions to affirm. That means you'll have to poke around for facts.

A final thought: Which of the four words comes easiest for you? Teaching and encouraging are usually easier, and that is where most mentors excel. But without reproof and correcting, mediocrity sets in. You cannot develop Christ-centered disciples unless you reprove and correct. Why? Think about your career: did you do your job's activities excellently the first time you tried them? Or did you perform better after someone who knew what they were talking about critiqued you and showed you how to improve?

Though lovingly confronting another believer involves risk, we are admonished by the Bible to do it. It is not optional. By avoiding the misconceptions and following the biblical guidelines, you can fulfill your mandate to "admonish one another." The risk is small compared to the rewards. Does one of your mentorees need a loving encounter with you to help him become more Christlike? Do you love him enough to mention it?

CHAPTER ELEVEN

Keep the Third Generation in Mind

WHAT IS THE GOAL OF ONE-TO-ONE MINISTRY? IS IT TO reach the second spiritual generation—mentor to mentoree? That's a noble start, but we cut the process short unless our mentorees are faithfully reaching and discipling the people in "their" world—the third spiritual generation. That will take longer than a six-week discipleship course or a twelve-week group Bible study. Looking to the spiritual generation beyond your own mentorees is a different way of thinking. You can't be content merely to "have a ministry"!

Let's look at the ministry of Jesus: Which generation did He have His eyes on? In John 17, Jesus' famous final prayer—only a day before He was crucified—shows a "both-and" combination that is often overlooked:

"I ask on *their behalf*; I do not ask on behalf of the world, but of those whom You have given Me." (verse 9, emphasis added)

"I do not ask on behalf of these alone, but for those also who believe in Me *through their word*." (verse 20, emphasis added)

In verse 9 He is *not* praying for the world but for the disciples whom God has given Him—the Twelve and perhaps a few others. Then in verse 20 He prays for those who become believers *through* the Twelve—the third generation! He fully expects His disciples to be fruitful in bringing the gospel to others. His goal is bigger than mentoring the Twelve.

Reaching the third generation was in His mind from the beginning. It was never Jesus' intention to disciple one generation only, as seen in Mark 3:14: "And He appointed twelve, that they might be with Him, and that He might send them out to preach."

What about Paul? He too has the third (and fourth) generation in mind when he tells Timothy, "The things which you have heard from me in the presence of many witnesses, these entrust to faithful men who will be able to teach others also" (2 Timothy 2:2).

Discipling Timothy was not enough. Paul expected Timothy to pass on "the things" to faithful people, and for those faithful people to reach still others—spiritual reproduction.

Bible study groups often end with the second generation. Sometimes the same eight Christians study together for years and never entertain the idea of breaking up to start new studies or inviting others to join—after all, others wouldn't "fit into our group." I applaud the honesty of one study member who said, "I like the fellowship and I don't want to go through the hassle of getting to know new people or starting over. Isn't it terrible to be that selfish? But that's how I feel." And so they go year after year feeding themselves. Our study groups have become swamps, not rivers.

Granted, some discipleship groups need to focus on the growth of the members for a time, particularly those with special needs or from dysfunctional backgrounds. But wouldn't the healing accelerate if the members reached out with the gospel?

As you disciple others, are you thinking of third and fourth spiritual generations? Often the answer is, "I'm struggling to get my mentoree to read the Bible consistently;

how can I think about him reaching someone else?" Good point. That's often how I feel. Even so, it's best to begin creating an atmosphere of outreach from day one. Here are a few ideas:

- As you pray with your mentorees, pray for your nonbelieving friends. They will catch on.
- Talk with them about their nonbelieving friends: What are they like? Where do they stand with the Lord? Pray together about them.
- Arrange for them to meet your nonbelieving friends and vice versa. It is amazing what synergistic relationships the Lord puts together.
- Sponsor an "Andrew dinner." Each protégé (or couple) invites two or three nonbelieving friends to a nice dinner with an interesting after-dinner speaker. The speaker relates his or her spiritual journey or presents a special topic addressing the spiritual needs of the group.

For example, Alma and I held an Andrew dinner one Christmas entitled "How a Submarine Driver and a Cheerleader Discovered the True Meaning of Christmas." Our speaker formerly served as an officer on a submarine, and his vivacious wife had been a school cheerleader. They described their Christmases without Christ and then contrasted that with what Christmas meant after they found Christ. It was a hit!

However, nothing can substitute for your zeal to reach others. If you genuinely long to reach nonbelievers, your people will catch on quickly. And you don't need the gift of evangelism to accomplish this—just a heart that wants "all to come to repentance" (2 Peter 3:9). If you are not interested in outreach, you will infect your mentorees with the same attitude.

It may be that one or two of your protégés possess the gift of evangelism. Use them as models for the others. What an exciting environment you will create!

Missionary statesman LeRoy Eims and I often talked about what made some Navigator ministries exciting while others seemed tired, even though they were led by mature believers. He said repeatedly, "Evangelism puts the fizz in the Coke! When the fizz goes out of the Coke, it is flat." Without an outreach mentality your ministry will become self-centered—no fizz! And if you don't bring it in early, you will have difficulty bringing it in later.

But wait a minute! If I'm not satisfied until I see the third generation, when will the discipling process end? I'll never finish! And how can I control the fruitfulness of my protégés? Good point. No one can guarantee that our protégés will be fruitful. And let's be realistic: who wants to enter into a discipling relationship if it means meeting weekly for the rest of our lives?

Discipling is similar to parenting. Does parenting ever end? Some parents foolishly think when their kids leave the house at age eighteen their parenting responsibilities are finished. What a glorious day that will be! Then comes the phone call from an eighteen-year-old: "We're thinking about marriage! No, I'll finish college. He's going to get a job at a tattoo parlor, and I'll go to school while he works. Money will be no problem—we're in love." When you heard the words *marriage* and *tattoo* in the same conversation, you knew parenting was not over!

So it is with discipling. Like parenting, it sometimes requires extreme attentiveness (rescuing toddlers from electrical outlets) and sometimes you can ease back (when they go to the grandparents' house for a week), and sometimes you must intervene with counsel (as in the marriage-tattoo illustration).

As the years go by, keep the friendships but alter the relationships. It may start with weekly meetings and high accountability, but as time passes that will need to be varied. And sometimes your mentorees need a break from you!

I have noticed that some of those with whom I had the most intense mentoring relationships seemed to tire of it after a while. So, like children, I let them go. I keep the friendship, but not intensely. But now I get letters of appreciation for what I "did for them." I limit my contribution to praying for them and giving occasional counsel when asked.

Like Jesus, plan your discipling with the third generation in mind. That involves more than a twelve-week program. It will require you to be wise in how you spend your discipling time so you don't burn out.

CHAPTER TWELVE

Running on a Cool Engine: Life Management Skills for Disciplers

DISCIPLERS GET TIRED. FACE-TO-FACE MENTORING MAKES a big demand on our time and emotions. We're giving our hearts, not just information. Not only that, but because disciplers are competent, we're also asked to lead ministries in church. Add in the demands we face in our career or running a home and raising kids, and it's no wonder we are tired! In desperately seeking rest, we are tempted to jettison personal ministry.

How can we find time for personal ministry when our days are winding tighter and tighter? A coworker was with me on a busy ministry trip. As we relaxed in the motel whirlpool late one evening after a long day of appointments, he complimented me on my endurance. "You seem to run on a cool engine," he said.

I'd never heard it put that way before, but because others have made similar comments, I investigated what I do and don't do that makes for a "cool engine." To my surprise I found out that few Christian leaders apply the following guidelines consistently. Perhaps these tips will help you run on a cool engine as you disciple others.

Learn to Say No

According to veteran missionary Skip Gray, "Not every bag that comes off the conveyor belt at the airport has your name on it." You don't need to meet with every person who wants a piece of you.

Have you noticed that Jesus sometimes said no to ministry opportunities? In Mark 1:36-38 the disciples were frantically searching for Him in the wilderness early in the morning. "Everyone is looking for You," they pleaded when they found Him. But rather than acquiesce to the demands of His disciples, Jesus went to the towns nearby, saying, "That is what I came for."

There's more. In John 7:1-9 Jesus' brothers wanted Him to go immediately to the feast at Jerusalem. Jesus said no. The man in Luke 8:27-39 whom Jesus healed of many demons "begged" to return with Jesus across the lake. Jesus said no.

Saying no to ministry opportunities does not mean you are hardhearted; you have only limited time. Use it wisely.

Not only must we learn to say no to ministry opportunities, we must also learn to say no in our careers. To quote Lee Iaccoca, "On his deathbed no one ever says, 'I wish I had spent more time at the office.'" You may need to make career sacrifices to have time to disciple others.

And finally, you may need to say no to your church! According to the 80/20 rule, 80 percent of the work in the church is done by 20 percent of the members. When the Sunday school superintendent is desperate for nursery workers, you get the phone call. Because you are conscientious, you may find it hard to say no. After all, your two children were cared for by others in the nursery not long ago. Then the superintendent says, "You're just the person we need! The nursery can't go on without you! It won't take much time . . . honest!" Hmmmm.

Keep Short Accounts with People

Nothing wears us out like conflicts with people. Long hours, impossible odds, challenging finances—none are as draining on Christian leaders as conflicts with people. And it is usually not our protégés or even nonbelievers, but fellow believers with whom we fight.

I once worked with an extremely talented co-worker, but after a year "Dean" (not his real name) seemed tired, touchy, and defensive. He was not the happy, joyful person I once knew, and I was beginning to resent him. I started having mental arguments with Dean at night as I lay in bed praying for sleep. I dreaded going to the office on days I was scheduled to meet with him. I was stressed. I needed a day off.

For Labor Day I decided to go bird-watching—a hobby that lets me forget the office and get lost in the wacky world of swamps and birds. I packed a lunch the night before, including a bird-watcher's breakfast—Hostess creme-filled cupcakes. I planned to leave at 5 A.M. and not return until dark. A whole day without Dean.

Early the next morning, in the darkness, before I turned the key in the ignition, I surrendered my stress with Dean to the Lord and asked God to give me a good day of relaxing. Off I went, sack lunch and breakfast in the back seat. Within five miles on a back road I saw a pair of bald eagles on a utility pole, majestic with the rising sun striking their white heads. What a find! But as I left the eagles I found myself meditating on Dean. Again I surrendered to the Lord—or tried to.

At a little roadside swamp a sora rail and a common snipe appeared. Talk about exciting! But soon Dean was back in my mind. He might as well have been in the back seat! By noon, I had identified forty-five species, but I'd identified Dean forty-five times too. Even though I kept turning Dean over to the Lord, I couldn't shake him. My day of refreshing was slipping through my fingers.

Lunchtime. I pulled up to the edge of a prairie to eat my lunch and see what birds would fly in. I tuned the radio to an easy listening station and prepared to enjoy a "Dean-less," worry-free lunch. But I wasn't prepared for the first song. It was Bobby McFerrin's hit, "Don't Worry, Be Happy."

"Easy for him to sing," I muttered, "He never had to work with Dean!" So I tried thinking happy thoughts.

Back to Dean. I tried not to think at all. More Dean. As I finished my sandwich, I admitted that relaxing wasn't the way to eliminate people stress. I knew what I had to do.

That night I wrote down my expectations for Dean and where I felt he was falling short. I also wrote down what I thought his expectations were of me and how I might be disappointing him. Then I prayed over both lists.

The next day Dean and I sorted it out. I confessed and he confessed in the spirit of Matthew 18:15. He also shared other battles he was fighting that I was unaware of.

"Birding with Dean" taught me the powerful lesson that trying to reduce stress without resolving interpersonal conflict is fruitless. Even though I had other heavy responsibilities that month, they were not as heavy as the unresolved conflict with Dean. Acts 24:16 guided me to talk with Dean: "I also do my best to maintain always a blameless conscience both before God and before men."

As the late Rod Sargent, former vice president of development for The Navigators, used to say, "It's not what you eat that makes you ill; it's what is eating you."

To keep your tank full, keep short accounts.

Avoid Energy-Sapping People (ESPs)

We are commanded to love everyone, but we need to wisely restrict the access we give those who destructively sap our energy.

Years ago one of the young couples Alma and I were discipling always seemed "down." We discovered finally that the wife and her mother talked on the phone several times a day and it usually ended in sharp words and bitter emotions. As we listened to the wife describe her mother we concluded she was a "holy ESP." Though a stalwart in their local church, she spewed venom on her children when they wouldn't take her advice.

Years ago, one of the men I was discipling seemed to wear me out. I returned from meetings with "Bob" emotionally depleted. Looking back I see that he had severe emotional wounding from his childhood, but I didn't know how to deal with it. So he talked about the same issues over and over. He needed more than I could give. I should have ended it sooner and referred him to a gifted counselor.

This is not an excuse to avoid those we don't like. But unless your ministry calling is to counsel ESPs you will only wear yourself out trying to meet their demands. Are there two or three someones in your life who constantly drag you down? Talk to them about it if you can, but if they continue to browbeat you, refer them to someone else.

Don't Try to Get Everything Done

Just because you write something on your weekly to-do list doesn't mean it has to get done! In many careers, such as sales, public relations, farming, or teaching, there is always one more task to do. The same is true in discipling.

Jesus didn't heal every sick person in Galilee! He didn't touch every child in the crowd. He didn't pause by every leper at the side of the road.

Since you know you can't get everything done, focus on top-priority items. Work on #1 until it is done or you can go no further, then go on to #2 until it is done, then #3, and so on. Obviously, interruptions will occur, but you get the idea. I like the words attributed to Dwight Eisenhower: "What is important is seldom urgent. What is urgent is seldom important."

If you are a perfectionist this will be tough. I find that praying through my "to-do list" for the upcoming day gives me a sense of God's hand on my life.

Limit Your Time Investment

A pastor's wife asked my advice about a woman in their church who was clamoring for one-to-one discipling. But Julie hesitated to train this aggressive leader. Why? She suspected the woman (though a dedicated Christian) wanted to meet with her for several years. "I can't commit to that!" Julie lamented. "I'm filled to capacity with relationships, but I feel guilty turning down such a rare opportunity."

I suggested she offer the young leader a six-week study—no promises—then renew it for another six weeks if it was working out. Julie was elated—a workable plan that didn't commit her to an open-ended relationship.

Another word of advice: be careful about adding new discipling responsibilities without dropping something else.

Distinguish Between Discipling and Counseling

Sometimes a protégé needs counseling, not discipling. There is a difference. In counseling you offer help for a specific issue. Your times together are aimed at solving a problem. It usually does not involve all of life, nor is reaching the third generation considered.

In discipling you occasionally play the role of counselor, but you will be drained if you try to disciple a person whose main need is counseling. I usually meet once or twice casually with a potential mentoree to determine whether he would be better served by a counselor.

Send Others in Your Place

The apostle Paul was pressed for time and couldn't visit Corinth conveniently, so he sent his mentoree, Timothy: "For this reason I have sent to you Timothy, who is my beloved and faithful child in the Lord, and he will remind you of my ways which are in Christ" (1 Corinthians 4:17).

This is another way to involve mentorees in ministry—send them to minister on your behalf. Timothy was a "little Paul" in that he was Paul's "beloved and faithful child in the Lord." Paul was confident Timothy would accurately represent him and, more important, Christ. Teach your mentorees to do the same.

Delegate

No one can do some tasks as skillfully as you. But if another can do it 80 percent as well, delegate it! Often we hesitate to delegate because the task is something we enjoy or because we are afraid. We keep it, not because someone else couldn't do it, but because of our own insecurity.

Even the great leader Moses struggled with delegation. In Exodus 18:13-23 he is confronted by his father-in-law, Jethro, who observed that Moses was the bottleneck as the Israelites lined up around him waiting their turn to receive his counsel. In verse 18 Jethro says, "You will surely wear out, *both yourself and these people* who are with you, for the task is too heavy for you; you cannot do it alone" (emphasis added).

Notice the phrase *both yourself and these people*. Some martyr-like leaders are willing to endure the long hours. But they fail to realize that the followers pay a price.

Jethro goes on to tell Moses to select godly men, place them over the congregation, and "let them judge," reserving only the hard cases for Moses. Could the godly men do the judging as well as Moses? Perhaps not, but Moses as the bottleneck was unacceptable. How else would his apprentices learn to become excellent judges?

I ask myself frequently, *Am I doing anything someone else ought to be doing?* And *Am I doing something that someone else can do better?* The words of Dawson Trotman haunt me: "Don't do anything that someone else *could do* or *should do*." That increases your capacity.

Stay Deep in the Word and Prayer

Once I was in Korea on an exhausting seven-week missions trip. I was at the mercy of my energetic Korean hosts, who kept me busy giving talks and meeting with growing young disciples. I loved it!

At first I ran on adrenaline from the excitement of being in Asia for the first time. But soon I began to wear out both physically and spiritually. I started looking for excuses *not* to serve my Korean hosts. That's when I realized my quiet times alone with God were inadequate for the amount of output I was giving.

But I fell into a trap! I focused on studying the Scriptures to find something "for others." I made sermons for others. Others were constantly on my mind as I meditated and prayed. I missed what God had for *me!*

At times we must prepare for others—a special Bible study, a key verse, or a question to ask. But, more important, set aside time to fill your heart with fresh insights just for you! Out of that will come blessing for others.

Disciplers do not have the privilege of skimping on time alone with God without consequences. Oh, we can get by for a time passing out old scriptural insights, but we will soon lose heart. Look at Jesus in Luke 5:16: "But He Himself would often slip away to the wilderness and pray." If the Son of Man needed secret times alone with the Father, how about you and me?

Note the word *often*. It was habitual. He did it frequently. Note the words *slip away*. He didn't announce it; He just did it. And note where He went—to *the wilderness*. He was alone, in solitude—not around people. And what was He doing in the wilderness? Praying.

What a powerful example! Even though secret prayer requires concentration, it refreshes the heart. But today we are constantly with people, constantly engaged, constantly plugged in. It is time to head for the wilderness.

Lately, I've been taking two hours occasionally on Sunday afternoons to drive out on the prairies east of town to be alone with the Lord. It's not exactly wilderness, but I've got a couple of favorite lonely places. At first I used the time to plan ministry, intercede in prayer, and organize the upcoming week, but something was missing. I was demotivated, even though I was trying to follow Jesus' example. So I put away my Day-Timer and prayer requests and simply enjoyed reading wherever I felt like in the Bible, stopping to meditate, praise, and give thanks to God.

What a lift! I came back with nothing to show for my two hours in the wilderness—not even a Bible study for a mentoree—but it was great. I simply enjoyed being with God.

I like to have a focused time of solitude with God once a day for twenty to sixty minutes, once a week for two hours, and once a year for four days. How about you? Are you alone with the Lord enough?

Take Time Off, Even When You Are Busy

We all know the value of a day off. God Himself set the example by working six days and resting on the seventh. But many Christians are not resting on the seventh or the sixth. Instead we frantically fill the weekend trying to catch up on all the stuff we've let go.

Or we work hard to enjoy leisure. It's off to the mountains to enjoy the cabin. Once there, we work like crazy to fix the leaky roof, then come back Sunday night exhausted.

Or to make sure our kids are not deprived, we enroll them in gymnastics, baseball, piano lessons, and Brownies—all at the same time. Not only do we get tired chauffeuring them all over town, but they get tired too. One little guy told his mom, "Why can't we just stay at home one night?" Kids shouldn't be programmed all the time, and neither should you.

What about the busy times of the year? We know we should take a day off each week, but when it's "crunch time" we skip our Sabbaths. True, some months of the year are busier than others. But the Israelites faced that too. God's word to them in Exodus 34:21 was: "You shall work six days, but on the seventh day you shall rest; even during plowing time and harvest you shall rest."

Even during plowing time and harvest! Farmers know they must get the planting and harvesting done during good weather. Miss those "crunch times" and there will be no crop. But Exodus says we are to rest during busy times as well.

I admired my father in that regard. Though the neighbors might be plowing on a warm, dry Sunday in April if rain was expected on Monday, my dad would not. And God blessed him nicely in his fifty years of non-panic farming. If you don't take a rest until you are burned out, it will be too late. Rest before you think you need rest. When was the last time you had an uninterrupted hour of solitude with no agenda? The poet George Herbert said it well: "By all means use sometimes to be alone. Salute thyself; see what thy soul doth wear."[1]

Reduce Your Technological Availability

To illustrate how far technology has gotten us, a friend in his Christmas letter facetiously listed his home address, business phone, home phone, fax number at work, fax number at home, pager number, business e-mail address, home e-mail address, business cell phone, and his personal cell phone—we have no excuse to be out of touch. Then he listed his wife's business phone, cell phone, home e-mail address, business e-mail address, business fax, and pager number. It took half a page.

Last week in a church service of seven hundred Presbyterians, a cell phone went off and wouldn't stop until the frantic owner found it. At management meetings it is common for cell phones to erupt and send their owners scurrying to the door whispering, "Hello! Hello!"

Unless you are a doctor or fireman on call, will there really be serious danger to anyone if you can't be reached for an hour or two? Alma and I were out to supper with friends who accepted cell phone calls during our meal together. A medical emergency? A dying parent? A real estate closing? No, their daughter was tired of the babysitter and wondered when the parents were coming home! We felt like we were interrupting their lives. I offer a couple of suggestions:

First, turn off your cell phone. Not just during church, but all the time. Use it for outgoing calls only. It was only a few years ago that we somehow survived without being available 24/7.

Second, just because e-mail is instantaneous, you needn't give an instantaneous response. Let it sit. Answer when it is appropriate.

Technology is wonderful, but make it serve you. Don't become a slave to something that has only been around for two-tenths of 1 percent of recorded history.

A closing story: A few years ago I was on the phone complaining to Adrian, a colleague, about how busy I was. "Honking at my taillights!" I said. "Too much to do and not enough time."

Silence. I waited, eager for the call to end so I could get back to my to-do list.

Adrian was breaking a custom. Usually when Christians tell Christians how busy they are, the listener responds by describing how much busier they are, which prompts the original busy person to out-busy the other. *Busyness face-offs*, I call them.

Silence. Adrian was not playing the busyness face-off game.

Finally he spoke: "Got a verse for you," he said. "Oh great!" I thought. "A Bible verse to patch my shattered nerves." I steeled myself for the homily on serenity that was sure to follow.

"Go ahead," I said halfheartedly. "What's the verse about me being too busy?"

"First John 1:9," he deadpanned.

Recognizing the passage immediately, I was stunned. "If we confess our sins, He is faithful and righteous to forgive us our sins and to cleanse us from all unrighteousness."

Did Adrian think I was sinning because I had too much on my plate? Didn't he know the work had to be done? That we were behind schedule? That's not a sin — just a way of life from which there is no escape.

"Thanks," I replied weakly. "That helps."

That conversation was years ago, but it was a wake-up call. I realized I had lost the peace that I had found as a new believer. I'd fallen into the trap of busyness and stress. But from that phone call I decided not to live that way any longer by the grace of God.

If you are serious about discipling others, you need to run on a cool engine with your tank full. Slow down — you're going too fast. Take heed to thyself! A frantic life is not attractive to your watching nonbelieving friends or to your mentorees. Do you want them to copy you?

It is not a sin to take heed to yourself so you don't burn out. Be attentive to the tiny air leaks in your energy that will give you a flat tire!

CHAPTER THIRTEEN

Building an Environment
of Grace

NOW IT IS TIME TO TALK ABOUT A DANGER IN DISCIPLING others, especially when you start to succeed. This danger is like carbon monoxide—you cannot detect it even when you're surrounded by it. But it is there. Outsiders sense it. But not you. How does it happen?

When you teach high biblical standards in discipleship (which you should) and if you lovingly confront sinful behavior (which you should), you are in danger of a "pushback" toward legalism. Any good emphasis, if overdone, can create an unhealthy atmosphere. Your biblical teaching can become a set of rules such as "You must have a quiet time every day," or "You must get counsel from your mentor before you make decisions," or "You must use a certain type Bible," or "You must pray a specific way." Without realizing it, mentorees can become legalistic and performance oriented in order to please you or "the group." Instead of Christ being central to the fellowship, members compete with one another. Sometimes a critical spirit toward outsiders, churches, and eventually one another, sets in. Behind the smiling faces, "heart problems" toward others increase.

For example, a high-accountability ministry can unwittingly produce believers who:

- are afraid to share their lives at the Bible study group for fear of looking bad.
- try to outdo one another in Bible study, Scripture memory, or sharing their faith.
- never let their hair down — never become vulnerable to others.
- never take risks because they are afraid of making a mistake.
- view the Christian life as following a series of guidelines rather than experiencing Christ daily.
- "perform" for the approval of their mentors.

None of this is anything you intended — it just happens as ministries succeed, often in the third generation. The scary truth is that any successful ministry can move in this direction unless action is purposely taken to avoid it. When the Enemy of our Soul cannot convince believers to renounce Christ, he will draw them toward legalism and performance.

The solution is not to renege on the wonderful biblical values you are building into the lives of the growing believers. Lowering your standards will not guarantee an environment of grace — and you'll get mediocrity instead. What can you do to maintain high biblical standards *and* develop an environment of grace? I have six suggestions.

1. Accept People As They Are
Romans 15:7 puts us all on level ground: "Wherefore, accept one another, just as Christ also accepted us to the glory of God."

I have no choice! I must accept others if I claim to have been accepted by Christ. Nothing communicates "non-grace" like making others feel unaccepted. Accepting another demands that I not subtly try to remake that person into someone I want him to be. We must take people as they are, since that is how Christ takes them. We dare not say, "Lord, as soon as You fix Jerry up a little, I'll accept him!"

Recently I went to a downtown city mission on a Sunday morning where about twenty-five to thirty broken people gathered—people who were open about their struggles with drinking, drugs, and addiction. As I was introduced to these struggling believers they welcomed me warmly and hugged me. I felt their acceptance. It was attractive. I felt free with them.

Why? The problem-plagued believers at the mission were so grateful God accepted them that they accepted me with open arms, and I "experienced" the grace they extended.

Destitute people sometimes come to a church looking for the pastor. A man I'll call Greg showed up at an inner-city church parsonage late one night—dirty, smelly, and high on cocaine. But he wanted help.

Burt, the renter who lived in the parsonage (not the pastor), welcomed Greg that night as a fellow sinner and began a friendship. Over the next couple of years, Burt led Greg to Christ and discipled him. Today Greg runs a Christian rehabilitation home for drug addicts, winning them to Christ and discipling them.

In recalling why he responded to Burt, Greg said that Burt *accepted* him just as he was that first night—dirty, smelly, and high. Though today these men have high standards in their disciple-making ministry (I know—I've been with them), they and their teams accept people just as they are in the midst of high standards. You can do it too.

2. See the Potential

Often leaders see people's liabilities rather than their potential in Christ. Isn't it true that when we meet a stranger we sometimes say to ourselves, "She'll never make it—not with that background" or "He'll never be a leader—he's too sensitive"?

When we telegraph silent judgmental thoughts to mentorees, they will never rise above our negative judgments. When Jesus looked upon the harassed multitudes in Matthew 9:36-38 He said, "The *harvest* is plentiful" (emphasis added). When I see the harassed multitudes, do I see a harvest? Do I see what people can become—or am I stuck on what they are?

Years ago a mother left her son in charge of his little sister, Sally. In his mother's absence the lad discovered some bottles of colored ink, opened them, and began to paint his sister Sally's portrait. You can imagine the mess—ink spattered everywhere.

His mother returned and saw the mess, but said nothing. She deliberately went over to the "drawing" the boy had made. She picked it up and said, "Why, it's Sally!" and she stooped down and kissed her son—Benjamin West! As an adult and famous landscape painter, Benjamin West was fond of saying, "My mother's kiss made me a painter."

Accept others as they are and see the potential for what Christ can make of them, and you are on your way to an environment of grace.

3. Be a Good Listener

We talked about listening in chapter 7, but it's so important that I want to mention another point here. Most spiritual leaders are prolific talkers! They thrive on preaching, exhorting, and wordiness. They are used to having the platform and being in control.

Though it seems you are not in control when you are listening, you might be surprised. Listening is a powerful ministry tool. It communicates that you are taking the talker seriously. You are giving honor. You are extending grace. That is attractive. They will come back to hear you listen to them again! In some ways, listening is more powerful than speaking.

4. Be Vulnerable

I've made errors on this one. For years I determined not to look bad in front of my mentorees. I wasn't trying to give the impression that I had it all together—I knew I didn't—but it often appeared that way. Even though I joked about committing a sin once twenty-five years ago, no one laughed. I instinctively never let anyone in close enough to see the real me.

A few years ago I goofed up in the presence of a co-worker I was informally mentoring named Jeremy. It was an obvious mistake and I couldn't weasel out of it. I was caught. For a moment there was silence. Then Jeremy started laughing—hard! He couldn't stop. Embarrassed, I asked why my error brought him so much mirth. Choking back laughter, Jeremy said, "Scott, it's good to know you're human like me!"

My accidental vulnerability was more encouraging to Jeremy than all my sermonettes. I didn't recognize the pressure incurred by a mentoree when his mentor is not vulnerable. There were many times over the years I could have confessed to Jeremy my fears, my temptations, and my worries, but I only shared a little so as to appear normal. I was mildly transparent, perhaps, but all the while my lack of vulnerability was portraying to Jeremy a warped view of life in Christ.

Was Jesus vulnerable to His disciples? Yes, in the Garden of Gethsemane. Was Paul vulnerable to Timothy? Yes—in 2 Timothy 3:10 he said, "But thou hast *fully known* my doctrine, manner of life...[and] longsuffering" (KJV, emphasis added). Paul didn't hide his life from Timothy.

Being vulnerable means giving others the tools they could use to hurt you if they chose to. Jeremy could have thrown my goof-up back in my face and still could to this day. Vulnerability means you could get hurt. It is more than being transparent. Publicly announcing you make a mistake now and then may bring a smile from your mentorees and a smirk from your spouse, but that is not being vulnerable. Allow people to get close enough to hurt you. Take off the mask. Hearts will be drawn toward you.

5. Be Generous and Hospitable

I learned this, too, by accident. A few years ago, a fellow missionary complimented me on how much he and others enjoyed coming to our home in Minneapolis for picnics, mini-seminars, and just hanging out. Why? Alma and I felt we did nothing special for these casual get-togethers. I forgot about the compliment.

Then recently, he and I were discussing what made an attractive ministry environment. He brought up the picnics at our house in Minneapolis. What made them good? His answer shocked me: "We got seconds on ice cream bars!"

That little touch of generosity (from our precious ministry funds!) made him and his friends feel honored. Grace was extended via ice cream bars!

Extending grace need not be opulent. I have felt grace from a financially strapped mission in the Caribbean where I was giving a seminar. They did the best they could for me in providing small but clean accommodations, feeding me meager but healthy food, and seeing that my needs were taken care of. It was far from opulent, but I felt like a king!

6. Have Fun

Here is a classic bit of evangelical history. Betty Skinner was a young, energetic Louisiana girl who worked in the office with Dawson Trotman in the late 1940s and 1950s. Dawson was known for driving himself hard, and he expected hard work from others. Betty told me of working long hours into the night with a small team of Navigators to meet deadlines. She also said it was challenging to be around Dawson because he held strict standards of excellence and was quick to point out errors.

"Why did you continue?" I asked Betty. "Why submit to such torture?" I expected her to draw a deep breath and think for a few seconds before answering. But she replied immediately and simply: "It was fun!" she said, with a Louisiana twinkle in her eyes.

How can you develop an atmosphere of fun? As Dwight Moody told a group of young, earnest pastors who wanted his advice on how to make their prayer meetings more interesting, "You might try being more interesting yourselves!" So if you desire an enjoyable atmosphere in your mentoring, you might try being more enjoyable yourself!

Not long ago I was ending a meeting with two younger staff on my development team. I was at the flip chart preparing to tear down three pages of notes we had scribbled. As Sharon conscientiously summarized the meeting, I tried to quietly tear the flip chart pages as I listened. But they wouldn't come off! My tearing was becoming louder, but all the while I was trying to give attention to Sharon's summary.

Finally, I lost it. I ripped at the stubborn sheets with flailing arms and put up a mock fight with the flip chart stand. Then I grabbed the sheets like a madman and mangled them into a great wad and deposited it on the table. Then, panting, I stared at my companions, who by this time were staring at me with their mouths open in disbelief. Silence.

Then George broke into laughter and said, "That's why we love working with you, Scott, because of stuff like that." And he motioned to the crumpled pile of former Canadian trees lying dead on the table. Then we all laughed. Sharon never finished her summary.

Enjoy life yourself. You'll pass it on to others. Remember that "a merry heart doeth good like a medicine" (Proverbs 17:22, KJV).

Creating a community of grace does not mean you can no longer hold people accountable. Nor does it imply that you have to smile and go along with every goofy idea your followers dream up. It does mean you have to be genuine, and that you need to examine the type of atmosphere you are creating. If the carbon monoxide is there, you may not know it until it is too late.

But take heart! As you genuinely walk with Jesus and stay close to your mentorees, you will develop a community that extends grace—and you probably won't even be aware of it. That is something God does.

Two Final Thoughts

Okay! You made it! Good job. As you prepare to launch out in discipling for the first time or as you continue discipling for the fiftieth time, keep 2 Corinthians 1:24 in mind: "Not that we lord it over your faith, but are working with you for your joy."

First, don't dominate your mentorees, but do all you can to help them find joy in God. When you assist another to increase his joy in God, you have been faithful. Well done, good and faithful servant. Keep on in Christ.

Secondly, the assumption I've made throughout these pages is that personal ministry is only effective under the leading of the Holy Spirit. I'm sure you believe that too, but let's agree to keep Him central no matter what the stage of ministry. Remember to rely on the One who said, "apart from me you can do nothing" (John 15:5).

Appendix

Most disciplers have in mind a few crucial topics they want to cover with mentorees. But *how* to share those key topics in an intriguing way in less than sixty minutes—there's the challenge! As I anticipate meeting with a mentoree, I usually have a topic idea, but too often I organize my game plan while dodging traffic en route to our get-together. Though I'm spontaneous by nature, I admit that mentoree sessions are more effective if I have a "pass-on-able" prepared ahead of time. But who has time to prepare a mini-sermon or Bible study?

Here are a handful of "sixty-minute pass-on-able teachings" to review with your mentorees. I call the format QPEA:

- Question
- Passages (key Scriptures)
- Example (from the Scriptures or your own life)
- Application

You can do the QPEA in any order, but starting with a provocative question and ending with application is usually best.

Adapt the QPEA to the needs of your mentorees. Go deeper by adding more verses, character studies, topical studies, or illustrations. Some can be broken into two or three sessions.

Launch into the QPEA after you have exchanged news and other pleasantries, and do it only if your mentoree does not have an urgent issue she needs to talk about. I introduce the QPEA with the comment, "Got an interesting question for you today!"

Also included in this appendix is a blank QPEA you may use to develop your own. Try them! Beats scrambling for Scriptures as you dodge traffic!

Pass-on-able Teachings (QPEA) for Stage Two (Discipling)

- Assurance
- Devotional life
- Sexual temptation
- How to handle money
- Giving (to whom)
- Giving (how much)
- Scripture memory
- Meditating on God's Word

Pass-on-able Teachings (QPEA) for Stage Three (Equipping)

- Bitterness, regret, and disappointment
- Why am I committing the same old sins?

Assurance of Salvation

Question: Which can you say with more certainty: that you are going to heaven when you die, or that you will make it home from this restaurant tonight?

Doesn't it seem arrogant for a person to be so sure he is going to heaven? Does it seem too simple?

Passage: 1 John 5:11-12 (meditate)

- According to this passage, what does it take to *have* eternal life?
- What does it take to *have* Christ?
- What would a person have to do to *lose* eternal life?

Example: A child may stray from a father's love but can never cease being the child of the father. The relationship may be estranged, but the fact of parenthood has not changed.

John 10:27-29 — Let's walk through this astonishing statement phrase by phrase. Was Jesus serious when he said, "never perish"? Does this mean physically?

Example: Suppose this ballpoint pen I hold in my hand represents you. The text says that "no one shall snatch them out of My hand." Then verse 29 says "No one is able to snatch them out of the Father's hand." Now wrap your hand around my hand. Do you see? The Father (your hand) holds Jesus (my hand) and Jesus holds you (the pen). Wriggle your hand. He is not about to let us get away. Not only that, but the Holy Spirit indwells us (pull the pen apart and produce the insert). (Look up Ephesians 1:13.)

Application: Ask your mentoree, "How sure are you of eternal life? 50 percent? 75 percent? 98 percent?" If not sure, ask, "Did you notice I didn't give you the choice of 100 percent? Would you say you have the Son? What makes you say yes or no? If God were to say at the end of your life, 'Why should I let you into my heavenly kingdom?' what would you say? Would you like to make sure right now?"

Additional Scriptures:

| John 1:12 | Ephesians 1:13-14 |
| John 5:24 | Ephesians 2:8-9 |

Devotional Life

Question: What keeps believers from getting into the Bible and praying daily? Discuss various obstacles we all face, like:
—I don't have time.
—It's hard to understand the Bible.
—I tried it once, but it didn't work.
—My life is so demanding.
—I don't know where to start.
—I don't get anything out of it.

Passages: Meditate on the following passages that show the devotional habits of Jesus and David.
Psalm 5:3   Psalm 27:1   Luke 5:16

Example: Jesus had a busy lifestyle with lots of demands; let's look at one day in His life in Mark 1:21-34. Read the passage and discuss the draining emotional and physical demands on Jesus. Then meditate on verse 35.

Example: Explain the benefits and costs *you* have realized by having regular devotions.

Application: What hindrances do you face in getting into the Bible and praying every day? When during the day would be the best time? Where would be the best place to have it? How long would you realistically be able to take? What would you do in your quiet time? Where in the Bible would you read? Do you know how to pray using the ACTS guide? (Adoration, Confession, Thanksgiving, Supplication)

Let's have a fifteen-minute quiet time together right now. Here's how I do it. Let's read Mark 1:1-13. I'll read three verses, then you read three. OK? Ask, "What can we learn about Jesus from this passage? What stands out to you in this passage?" Pray together alternately. Note: Be sure to stop at fifteen minutes.

Sexual Temptation
(Two or Three Sessions)

Question: One of the biggest temptations believers face is sexual impurity. But I take comfort in the fact that godly people in the Bible struggled with it too. What lessons can we learn from David and Joseph about sexual purity?

Example: David (2 Samuel 11, 12:1-14)
Read the passage, stopping now and then to comment. I like to ask the following questions:
- Do you think David had been on the roof "observing" previously?
- Didn't David have other wives? Why another sexual partner?
- What strikes you about David's response when Nathan confronts him?
- Review David's confession in Psalm 51.

Example: Joseph (Genesis 39)
- Could Joseph have avoided this frame-up?
- What lessons can we learn about sexual purity from Joseph?

Passages:
Proverbs 7:6-27
Matthew 5:27-28
1 Thessalonians 4:3-8

Application: What stands out to you in these passages? What commitments can you make or what actions must you take to stay sexually pure?

How to Handle Your Money
(Two or Three Sessions)

Question: Is it wrong for Christians to become rich? Why or why not? What does the Bible say about money? Money is a crucial component of following Christ. Do you agree or disagree? What do you think of the comment attributed to J. D. Rockefeller when asked, "How much money is enough?" "Just one dollar more!" he replied.

Passage: 1 Timothy 6:6-10,17-19. Meditate on the passage and make observations.

- To whom is this teaching directed?
- Is the old adage "Money is the root of all evil" true?
- What is the significance of the word *wandered* in verse 10?
- What is the likely outcome for the person who wants to become rich?
- How should those who have wealth conduct themselves?

Additional References:
Psalm 37:21
Psalm 50:10-12
Proverbs 3:9-10
Proverbs 6:6-11
Proverbs 22:7
Haggai 2:8
Luke 12:15

Example: Luke 12:13-34 (Note: The oldest male typically inherited all the father's assets.)

Example: Share personal lessons you've learned in becoming a biblical steward of God's resources.

Application: What stands out to you from these passages? An action to start? Stop?

Giving: To Whom?
(Two Sessions)

Question: Where should a believer put his or her giving dollars? There are so many opportunities, so much fundraising—how does one know where to give in light of all the good ministries and church needs? Should it all go to the local church for distribution?

Passages: To what (whom) shall I give?
A. Ministers of the gospel
   1. Missionaries
        Luke 10:1-7
        1 Corinthians 9:14
        Philippians 4:15
        3 John 7,8
   2. Local assembly
        Deuteronomy 14:27
        Acts 2:44-45; 4:34-35
        Galatians 6:6
        1 Timothy 5:17
B. Needy believers
        Romans 12:13
        James 2:15-16
        1 John 3:17
C. The vulnerable
        Deuteronomy 14:28,29
        Deuteronomy 15:7-11
        Deuteronomy 24:19-22
        Luke 18:22

Example: Share your own example of where you give and why.

Application: What insights did you get from these passages? Where do you believe you should give?

Giving: How Much?

Question: How much does the average American give to charity? 1 to 2 percent of their annual income. On average, Christians give slightly more. How much should believers give? Ten percent?

Passages:
Deuteronomy 14:22   2 Corinthians 8:3
Deuteronomy 16:17   2 Corinthians 9:6-7
Malachi 3:8-10 (Note Malachi 1:8. The best lambs were to be given, not lame ones.)

Example: My mentoree, Robert, was a new believer earning $800 per month in take-home pay. The pastor of his church preached on tithing, and Robert said that if he tithed, that would leave $720 to provide for his family. His rent was $550; utilities $75. Other monthly expenses included the babysitter, gas to get to work, food for the family, clothes, insurance, and school supplies.

"Should I tithe?" he asked. "It seems like too much."

Two days later I was with another mentoree, a gifted stockbroker who earned $250,000 per year. If he had heard the message on tithing, he would have given $25,000 and then have to eke out a living on $225,000!

Because these meetings were only two days apart, I was struck by the notion that the "tithe" cannot be the only standard in giving. What do you think? If tithing is the rule, why did Jesus mention it only twice? Why doesn't Paul mention it at all?

What would you have told Robert?

Passage: I took Robert to Luke 21:1-4. Meditate on this passage and see if this is not a better answer than simply to "tithe."

Application: First Corinthians 16:2 seems to imply we should give by plan. Do you have a giving plan? If you are married, does your spouse agree with it?

How much do you think you should give?

Scripture Memory

Question: A believer stated, "I don't think it is necessary to memorize verses from the Bible; just to know generally what the Bible says is good enough. Agree or disagree?

Passages: Notice the phrase *I do not forget* and the word *remember* in these verses from Psalm 119:16,52,61,83, 93,109,153. Also see John 15:20 and Acts 20:35.

Meditate on

Deuteronomy 6:6-7	Psalm 119:9,11
Joshua 1:8	Colossians 3:16

Example: Meditate on Matthew 4:1-11. What was Jesus' view of memorizing Scripture?

Example: Has Scripture memory been of value to you?

Tips on Scripture memory:
1. Memorize every word. Each word is important.
2. Memorize the reference "fore and aft."
3. Memorize by the natural phrases of the verse.
4. Meditate on each word, emphasizing a different one each time you go over it.
5. Review your new verse every day for six weeks.
6. Say it aloud to a friend.
7. Write it out and pray through it.
8. Keep your verses with you and review them periodically.

Quote: "I know of no greater form of intake of the Word which pays greater dividends for the time invested than Scripture memory."   —Dawson Trotman, founder of The Navigators

Application: Show your mentorees how to memorize Scripture by doing it together. Start in the NavPress beginning Scripture memory packets, "Beginning with Christ" (five verses); next, "Going On with Christ" (eight verses); then graduate to "The Topical Memory System" (sixty verses).

Meditating on God's Word

Question: What small habit of the mind does the Bible say is the secret to prosperity?

Passages: To find the answer, work your way through these passages word by word:
Joshua 1:8-9
Psalm 1:1-3

Question: What is the result of meditation? Does it include material success? Eastern mystics use "meditation" and chant mantras; is this what the Bible has in mind? How would you define meditation as used in Psalms and Joshua? (Explain the rumination concept of animals with several stomachs, such as cows—burping back grass and chewing the cud to squeeze out more nutrients.)

Example: Together meditate on Philippians 4:6-7 using several techniques:
1. The vowel method (AEIOU).
  A—Ask questions.
  E—Emphasize key words.
  I—Say it in your own words.
  O—Other verses—what do they add?
  U—What is the application for *you* from this passage?
  Note: This is a wonderful way not only to show mentorees how to meditate but to learn how to occupy the mind with Scripture—it keeps a person from worry and other mental preoccupations.
2. Context. Paraphrase the verse before and after.
3. Pray through the verse together back and forth.

Application: What is the connection between meditation and Scripture memory? Any ideas on how you can put meditation into your life as a habit?

Bitterness, Regret, and Disappointment
(Dropping Baggage from the Past)

Question: Have you ever known bitter people? What are they like? Why have they become bitter? Is there a chance that you could become bitter as time passes?

Example: Review the stories of Esau, Naomi, and Joseph, then fill in the chart below.

Passage	Disappointments or Unfulfilled Expectations	Bitterness Symptoms	Bitterness Target
Genesis 27:41-46; 28:6-9			
Ruth 1			
Matthew 1:18-25			
Me			

Each character experienced disappointment. Is it possible to become bitter without a disappointment?
- What unfulfilled expectations (dashed dreams) accompanied Esau, Naomi, and Joseph?
- Does bitterness always require a target?

Passage: Meditate on Hebrews 12:15.

Example: Share your own temptations toward bitterness next to "Me" in the chart above. What lessons have you learned?
Ask your mentoree the same questions.

Application: What steps can we take to overcome bitterness or to ensure that it will not become part of our lives?

Why Am I Committing the Same Old Sins?

Question: Have you ever noticed that we believers are not immune to the same sins we committed in the days before we walked with God? Some temptations we struggled with long ago are still with us — like lust, greed, explosive anger, and insecurity. Why?

Passage: Discuss Romans 7:15-20.

- Paul was a mature believer when he wrote Romans, shouldn't he have victory by now?
- When Paul was converted on the Damascus Road, what in him was not changed?
- Would Paul say "the Devil made me do it" (verse 20)?
- Do you think our sin nature gradually gets better?

Example: Think about the following partial-truth analogy. Some Christians believe that our sin nature and our new nature are like two dogs fighting for possession of our hearts. The Christian strengthens the new-nature dog by feeding it the Word, by fellowshipping with other believers, and so on.

Conversely, you can defeat the evil-nature dog by starving it: don't feed it worldly lusts, don't yield to temptations. Gradually that mean, old-nature dog will be starved out and get weaker until it lies harmlessly whimpering in a small corner of your heart. Victory!

What truths and errors are contained in this analogy?

Passages:

    Romans 6:6-14   Colossians 3:1-8

    Romans 8:5-8   James 4:6-7 (first submit, then resist)

Application: Are you believing the lie that your sin nature is gradually getting better and better?

Note: To complete the dog analogy, I describe the sin-nature dog as being just as powerful as ever, but he is on a short chain and cannot harm us unless we foolishly go within range of his chain to befriend him (Romans 6:6-7). That seems more biblical.

Sample QPEA

Topic Title:_____

_____

Question to Discuss:_____

_____

Passages for Meditation:_____

_____

Notes:_____

_____

Example from Scripture:_____

_____

Example from Daily Life:_____

_____

_____

Application:_____

_____

_____

You have permission to reproduce this form for your personal discipling ministry.

The Wheel Illustration

This simple illustration has been used by The Navigators for more than fifty years to help Christians better understand what it means to live as disciples of Christ.

Question:
- What is a wheel like when it is out of balance?
- What parts of a wheel can people clearly see when it is turning rapidly—the spokes, or the center? Why is this important?
- What happens when a wheel with weak spokes hits a bump?
- Which is your strongest spoke? Weakest?

The Hub: Christ the Center
(2 Corinthians 5:17; Galatians 2:20)
Just as the driving force in a wheel comes from the hub, so the power for a believer comes from having Jesus Christ at the center of his or her life. The Holy Spirit empowers us to live for Christ.

The Rim: Obedience to Christ
(John 14:21; Romans 12:1)
The rim represents the believer's response to Christ's lordship through wholehearted obedience. The spokes show how Christ's power becomes operative in our lives.

Spoke: The Word
(Joshua 1:8; 2 Timothy 3:16)
The vertical spokes represent how we relate to God. God's Word is our spiritual food and our sword in spiritual battle. It is also our main means for discerning God's will.

Spoke: Prayer
(John 15:7; Philippians 4:6-7)
Through prayer we have direct communication with our heavenly Father and receive provision for our needs. Prayer also shows our dependence on Him and trust in Him.

Spoke: Fellowship
(Matthew 18:20; Hebrews 10:24-25)
The horizontal spokes represent how we relate to others — both believers and those who don't yet know the Lord. Christ-centered fellowship provides the mutual encouragement and stimulation we all need.

Spoke: Witnessing
(Matthew 4:19; Romans 1:16)
The natural overflow of a vibrant life in Christ should be sharing with others how they too can have this life. God has given believers the privilege of reaching the world with this good news.

Application: Pick one part of the wheel you'd like to strengthen in your life. What steps can you take?

Getting a Grip on God's Word

As Christians, we're convinced of the Bible's value in shaping our own lives and the lives of those to whom we minister. We know that "all Scripture is God-breathed and is useful for teaching, rebuking, correcting and training in righteousness" (2 Timothy 3:16, NIV).

But how can we get God's Word into our lives on a regular basis? What can we do to strengthen our grip on the Bible?

There are a number of ways we can expose our hearts and minds to the life-changing power of the Scriptures. The following illustration highlights five practical ways we can get a grip on God's Word.

All five methods are important. Try holding your Bible using just the hearing and reading fingers! Then add the study finger . . . better grip? Then add the memory finger. Finally, add the meditation thumb to get a good grip on the Bible!

The Hand Illustration

Question: What percentage can you recall of what you hear? (5-10%)? Read (10-15%)? Study (60%)? Memorize (100%)? Which is your strongest Bible intake finger and which is your weakest? Is it possible to excel in all five intake methods at once?

Hearing the Scriptures taught by others gives us the benefit of their thoughts and insights and stimulates our own appetite for the Word.

Reading the Bible gives us an overall picture of God's Word.

Studying the Scriptures leads us into personal discoveries of God's truths and helps us see how different parts of the Bible relate to one another.

Memorizing God's Word enables us to use the sword of the Spirit to overcome Satan and temptation. It also makes God's Word available to us at any time for witnessing or helping others to grow.

Meditation is used in conjunction with each of the other four methods. By meditating on God's Word—thinking about its meaning and how it applies to our lives—we can discover its transforming power at work in us.

The Bridge to Life

Step One:
God's Love and Plan

Us

God wants us to be His friend and to have a full life assured of His love.

Step Two:
Our Problem: Separation from God

Us
(Sinful)

God
(Holy)

We chose to disobey God and go our own willful way. We still make this choice today. The result is separation from God. On our own we cannot bridge the gap to Him.

Step Three:
God's Remedy: The Cross

Us
(Sinful)

God
(Holy)

Jesus Christ is the only answer to the problem of sin. He paid the penalty and bridged the gap between us and Himself.

Step Four:
Our Response

Are you here...   or here?

Us (Sinful)
• Sin
• Rebellion
• Separation

God (Holy)
• Peace
• Forgiveness
• Abundant Life

Believing means trust and commitment—acknowledging our sinfulness, trusting Christ's forgiveness, and letting Him control our lives.

Question:

Step One: When you think of God, what attributes come to mind?

Step Two: What is sin, really?

Step Two: What about "us" building our own bridge of a good life? (Ephesians 2:8-9)

Step Three: What does it mean to "believe"?

Step Three: What about all the hypocrites in Christendom?

Step Four: Is it possible to know for sure where you stand with God?

Step Four: What would keep you from crossing the bridge? Do you know how?

Gospel-Based Discipleship

Question: What is the difference in these two diagrams? Why are they important?

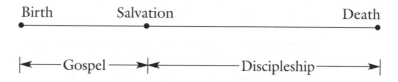

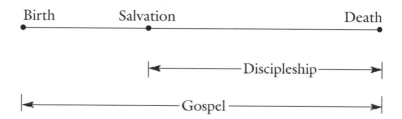

Passages: Based on the following passages, is the gospel a rational set of facts or more of a lifelong surrender? What is misleading about preaching a benefits gospel only?

1 Corinthians 15:3-4
Luke 19:1-10
Mark 8:34-38
Matthew 3:8-10
Luke 15:7

Example: How has a thorough understanding of the gospel's implications affected your growth in Christ?

Application: Are you preaching a benefits gospel only?

Quiet Times in Mark

"If you would be much like Christ."

Plan

A quiet time is time set aside to worship and learn from Christ.
Develop the habit of meeting with Him every day!
1. You'll need your Bible, a pen, and paper.
2. Before you read each day's Scripture segment, take a moment
   to acknowledge Christ's presence with you.
3. Read slowly, looking for "What is Jesus Christ like?"
4. Write down an original title for the Scripture segment (four
   words).
5. Write down two observations about Christ.
6. Application: Put down a brief answer to the question, "How
   can I apply this segment today?"

Sample

Mark 1:1-8

Title:
"One Mightier than I"

Observations:
1. Several names given Christ:
   a. The Son of God (verse 1)
   b. One Mightier than I (verse 2)
   c. The Lord (verse 3)
2. Christ is mightier than people.

Application:
I need to realize that Christ is mightier than all the people or
circumstances that will come my way today.

Schedule

(Just spend 10 minutes on one selection per day.)

Mark 1:1-8	Mark 6:1-13	Mark 10:1-12	Mark 13:1-13
1:9-15	6:14-29	10:13-16	13:14-23
1:16-28	6:30-44	10:17-22	13:24-37
1:29-39	6:45-56	10:23-31	
1:40-45		10:32-45	14:1-9
	7:1-23	10:46-52	14:10-21
2:1-12	7:24-30		14:22-26
2:13-17	7:31-37		14:27-42
2:18-28		11:1-11	14:43-52
	8:1-13	11:12-19	14:53-65
3:1-12	8:14-26	11:20-26	14:66-72
3:13-30	8:27-38	11:27-33	
3:31-35			15:1-15
	9:1-13	12:1-12	15:16-21
4:1-20	9:14-29	12:13-17	15:22-32
4:21-34	9:30-37	12:18-27	15:33-41
4:35-41	9:38-50	12:28-34	15:42-47
		12:35-44	
5:1-20			16:1-13
5:21-34			16:14-20
5:35-43			

My time:_____ My place: _____

Notes

Chapter 1

1. John Pollock, *Moody: The Biography* (Chicago, Ill.: Moody, 1963), p. 27.
2. Pollock, p. 27.
3. Pollock, p. 133.
4. Ralph Waldo Emerson, from *Essays: First Series. Friendship,* as quoted in *Bartlett's Familiar Quotations,* 16th edition (Boston: Little, Brown, 1992), p. 432.

Chapter 3

1. Michael Green, *Evangelism in the Early Church,* (London: Hodder and Stoughton, 1978), p. 173. Reproduced by permission of Hodder and Stoughton.

Chapter 4

1. E. Stanley Jones, *A Song of Ascents* (Nashville: Abingdon, 1968), p. 16.

Chapter 5

1 Jim Petersen, *Lifestyle Discipleship* (Colorado Springs, Colo.: NavPress, 1993), pp. 15-16.

Chapter 6

1. Phillip Keller, *A Shepherd Looks at Psalm 23* (Grand Rapids, Mich.: Zondervan, 1974), pp. 60-63.

Chapter 8

1. William J. Bennett, *The Moral Compass* (New York: Simon & Schuster, 1995), p. 657.

Chapter 12

1. Quoted in Thomas S. Kepler, *Pathways to Spiritual Power* (Cleveland: The World Publishing, 1952), p. 103.

Author

SCOTT MORTON serves as vice president of development for The Navigators. For fourteen years he led Navigator campus and marketplace ministries, in which he worked with students, businesspeople, and missionaries both stateside and overseas. He enjoys helping people grow in their spiritual journeys through small-group Bible studies and one-to-one mentoring. Scott has written numerous articles for *Discipleship Journal* and is the author of *Fund Your Ministry—Whether You're Gifted or Not* (Dawson Media). He and his wife, Alma, live in Colorado Springs, Colorado, and have two daughters, a son, and three grandchildren.

FUEL FOR THE RACE.

Spiritual Disciplines for the Christian Life

Drawn from Scripture and godly Christian lives, this
book serves as a guide to disciplines—Scripture
meditation, prayer, worship, fasting, solitude,
journaling—that can deepen your walk with God.

(Donald S. Whitney)

Soul Guide

Realize a deeper sense of spiritual direction and
guidance from biblical characters, contemporaries,
and Jesus' ministry.

(Dr. Bruce Demarest)

The River Within

Discover how to live life fully and passionately
through the soul-freeing love of the Trinity. This new
way of living will bring you closer to God as it
plunges you into the joy of living.

(Jeff Imbach)

To get your copies, visit your local bookstore, call
1-800-366-7788, or log on to www.navpress.com. Ask
for a FREE catalog of NavPress products. Offer #BPA.

NAVPRESS

BRINGING TRUTH TO LIFE
w w w . n a v p r e s s . c o m